THE
PROMISED
PARTY

Also by Jennifer Clement

Widow Basquiat: A Memoir
A True Story Based on Lies
The Poison That Fascinates
Prayers for the Stolen
Gun Love

THE
PROMISED
PARTY

Kahlo,
Basquiat
& Me

JENNIFER
CLEMENT

CANONGATE

First published in Great Britain, the USA and Canada in 2024
by Canongate Books Ltd, 14 High Street, Edinburgh EH1 1TE

Distributed in the USA by Publishers Group West
and in Canada by Publishers Group Canada

canongate.co.uk

1

For permissions credits, please see p. 283

British Library Cataloguing-in-Publication Data
A catalogue record for this book is available on
request from the British Library

ISBN 978 1 83885 927 5

Typeset in Minion by
Palimpsest Book Production Ltd, Falkirk, Stirlingshire

Printed and bound in Great Britain by Clays Ltd, Elcograf S.p.A.

Contents

PRELUDE   1

MEXICO CITY   13

Some Facts   15
Calle Palmas   16
Frijol   18
What Was Given   23
Ruth María Alvarado Rivera   26
Clásica Flor de Naranja Aguas de Colonia Sanborns   29
Everything Was What It Was   31
Chona   34
The ABC Hospital   38
Dandelions   40
Ballet   41
Encyclopedia   43
I Have Always Loved Stories About Orphans   45
'We have a long way to go'   48

She Taught Me to Be Afraid of Everything 52

The Water Diviner 54

Buttons 56

The Latest Fashion 58

Family Collage 59

Acapulco 61

The Parents Were Elsewhere 65

Teatro Iris 69

Blindfolded 71

Stay Quiet 75

The Legendary Children's Parties 77

The Edron Academy 80

In the Shadow of Shadows 82

Blanca and Her Chicken 84

1968 86

More About 1968 89

1969 93

Two Lost Friends 96

And More Things 98

Reading the Trees 99

The Parties Were Dangerous 100

Strangers 102

Chona Marries Fidel 104

The Parties of the Empire of the Illusion 106

Like a Bomb Leaving 110

Mexico's IX General Census of the Nation 1970 115

A Midsummer Night's Dream 116

Nothing Came In and Nothing Went Out   118

Pachita   121

The Santa Martha Prison   125

The Days of the Shared Suitcase   127

'*El Tiempo Que Te Quede Libre*'   131

Trotsky's Rabbits   134

Wande   141

Aline Davidoff Misrachi   142

Stories About Rings   144

'*¿Oye, como se dice* window *en inglés?*'   149

To Walk Alone   151

Waldeen and 'The Dance of the Disinherited'   153

The Days of the Peppermint Frappé   158

The Decision of the Flower   163

Irene de Bohus   166

A Murder and Everything Is in Fours   168

There Was No Elsewhere   171

NEW YORK CITY   173

'I stabbed her but I never meant to kill her'   175

She Was the Kind of Woman Who Was Always Fainting   177

A Dancer in New York   179

Dreaming and Nightmaring   181

'Revolting Music'   183

Downtown Etiquette   187

Two Shadowmen   189

'Fuck Art Let's Dance'   191

Querencia   196

Valentine's Day Chocolates   200

Poetry Nights   201

Box for One Sock Found   204

TV Party   206

Tetracycline   208

People Who Are Not in This Book   213

Curare Poison   215

A Song   221

Paris 1   222

Paris 2   224

Paris 3   227

Paris 4   229

Lightning Strikes Again   230

Widow Basquiat   233

'*¿Dolor o placer?*'   238

Polaroids   241

La Tulipe   244

Walls Were Paper and Trains Were Books   247

D&G Bakery   251

An Incident on the Way to a Borges Reading   255

Night-time Phone Calls   257

I Say to You Goodbye   259

Four Paid Mourners   262

'Headless Body Found in Topless Bar'   264

Refrigerator   269

In Memory of Joan   271

Packing the Bags   274

Jean-Michel Basquiat 1960–1988   276

And Fate's Third Chance   278

Return   280

Permission Credits   283

Prelude

I was strange to myself. Slept uneasy. I walked between raindrops. The field came in the open window. As a child in Mexico City, I had dreams about a suitcase filled with candy. My hands were deep inside pockets, so I never held a hand to cross a street.

In 1978, at the age of eighteen, I left Mexico and went to New York City, where it seemed as if everyone had taken the exit door or was kicked out. Some of us were throwaways. We never spoke the words 'return' or 'go back' and we were not missing. All of us were some sort of runaway. Even if we'd come from Mexico, Ohio, Canada, Michigan, Tunis or Cuba, we felt we were born from the subways and skyscrapers. The Island of Manhattan belonged in our passport.

'How did you come to be here?' we asked each other.

These were some answers:
'There's the door. It's there, staring at you all day long.'
'You don't go home even if you're cold.'
'It was like carousel music calling, calling and calling.'

And, in the beginning of those New-York-City-runaway, love-your-heart-out days, when no one knew AIDS was coming, I could kiss someone I didn't know. I could love a stranger.

• • •

I called her 'Minnie Mouse'. The first time I met Suzanne Mallouk she was wearing a black-and-white polka dot dress and her big greenish brown eyes made her look just like the cartoon character. Inside her tall, teased-up, beehive hairdo, held together by dozens of bobby pins, she hid her small bags of drugs.

Suzanne left her home in Ontario, Canada, and bought a one-way ticket to New York City. She emphasised 'one-way', as if 'one-way' were a destination, should be a place on a map.

Suzanne and I would go dancing, or to watch bands at the Mudd Club downtown. We dressed in black dresses, black stockings and black lace gloves. These were our night-time come-here, dare-me costumes.

Late, after clubbing, Suzanne and I would take a taxi down to the docks and the Fulton Fish Market at the South Street Seaport. In our high heels, we walked around and looked into the barrels and huge tubs filled with fish, crabs and shimmering squid. We came to know many of the fishermen. They were polite and a few joked around and asked us to marry them.

Soon after Suzanne had run away from home in 1980, she met Jean-Michel Basquiat, who was living on a stone bench in Washington Square Park with a blue wool blanket. His nickname for her was always Venus. Jean-Michel moved from the bench into Suzanne's small apartment on 1st Street and Avenue A, where he painted some of his early work.

When Jean-Michel did not come home at night, and even disappeared for a few days, Suzanne would spend most of her time looking for him. I would go with her, a love shadow, skipping from one club to the next. When we did find Jean-Michel at Mr Chow's or at Kiev's eating a large potato pancake with apple sauce, he was always happy to see us. Suzanne would sit on his lap and Jean-Michel would feed her like a child. He held up a spoon and told her to open her mouth. Say, 'Ahhh.'

When Jean-Michel moved out of Suzanne's apartment a year or so later, the wood floor was completely covered with a thick coating of his paint drippings, stains, spray and splatters. Hardened oil stick and melted crayons were embedded in the cracked floorboards and deep in the wood grain.

With Jean-Michel gone, Suzanne decided to paint. She threw away almost everything in her small apartment to make room for her art supplies and canvases; she only kept her bed and kitchen table with two chairs. We placed books, some clothes and an old toaster in the dumpster on the street, as well as four pairs of Jean-Michel's old shoes. I kept her large hardcover book on palmistry. We also threw away dozens of large rolled-up paper drawings by Jean-Michel.

Even before these housecleaning days, in a fit of rage at Jean-Michel, Suzanne once threw some of his sketches, smudged all over by his painted footprints, out of the kitchen window onto the roof next door. That afternoon there was a fierce New York City windstorm and I watched Jean-Michel's large sheets of drawing paper blow away like mangled wings.

Suzanne and I would walk down to fire-engine red Pearl Paint, the art store on Canal Street where she went to buy her canvas, oil stick and acrylic paints.

It was one-stop shopping at Pearl Paint as, conveniently, there was a regular dealer hanging out outside the store or sitting on the steps. He was tall and pale and sold small glassine envelopes of cocaine. He called me 'Little Baby' and called Suzanne 'Big Baby', as she always wore enormous, men's blue-jean overalls, which had belonged to Jean-Michel and were still covered in his paint. She cinched the overalls at the waist with a brown leather belt. This was her painting outfit.

The place was its own scene. The store was five storeys tall, with steep staircases, and we always ran into someone. Once, when we were in the checkout line behind the artist Vito Acconci, we watched him buy small bags of lime-green sequins to stick on his body. He kept asking the cashier, 'Are you sure this glue will wash off in the shower?' The cashier didn't know.

Julian Schnabel was there one day and Suzanne grabbed my wrist when we saw him walking in the front door. We ran up two flights of stairs and hid behind some shelves covered in paintbrushes. Crouching on the ground, Suzanne said, 'Keep quiet. He can't know I'm painting.' Suzanne didn't want anyone to know. It was our secret.

We were at the 1st Street apartment together many nights a week, usually after our waitressing shifts or after clubbing. We drank gold apple juice from her refrigerator covered in Basquiat's paint strokes, words, symbols and doodles. In her small apartment space, it was both a refrigerator and a closet. Inside was a tin of Maxwell House coffee, a plate with more than twenty thin, black rubber jelly bracelets and a small stack of papers with drafts of my poems beside a couple of cans of

Tab and a pile of paid Con Edison light bills. The plastic tray for eggs contained earrings and eggs.

A pair of Jean-Michel's lace-up leather ankle boots were under the small white kitchen table with some red socks still stuffed inside. He'd also left behind two Lee J. Ames's *Draw 50* 'how-to' drawing books. One was *Draw 50 Famous Faces* and the other was *Draw 50 Famous Cartoons*, with Yogi Bear, Fred Flintstone and Felix the Cat inside.

While Suzanne painted, I sat at the kitchen table with a notebook and pencil. I was handwriting dozens of made-up stories to sell to true-confession magazines. I wrote: 'What Really Happens Behind Closed Doors: A Las Vegas Maid Tells All Her Secrets'; 'I Found Love in the Arms of a Young Rock Star'; 'The Girl Who Could See Tomorrow'; 'Frustrated Twin Admits: My Sister Tried to Steal the Man I Love'; and 'It Didn't Take Me Long to Fall in Love with My Gardener'. Then, for days back at my own apartment at 13 St Mark's Place, I'd type up the stories on my electric Olivetti typewriter. It took me only eleven days to write my two romance novels, *The Labyrinth of Love* and *Desire Among the Statues*, which I sold for $500 each. I used to make up lists with the clichéd formula the editors wanted for these stories and romances so the writing would move more quickly.

List One: Colors for Lips
Snow White Apple Red
Sunset Red
Red Wine Red
Lollipop Red
Cherry
Red Hot Red

List Two: Plot Outlines
I hate you
I love you
I hate you
I love you

List Three: How to Create Passionate Tension
Don't
Yes
Don't
Yes
Yes
Yes

While I wrote poems or these stories and novels for cash, Suzanne painted George Washington as a black man on a dollar bill in a kinship with Jean-Michel's untitled green-and-yellow painting of ten dollars with a portrait of Hamilton. Suzanne also painted the cartoon figures of Black Dagwood and Blondie as well as large portraits of Malcom X and Muhammad Ali.

When Jean-Michel and Suzanne had lived together, he'd taught Suzanne about Vodou. As his father was Haitian, he felt connected to the ancestral spiritual ideas but it was both a joke and not a joke to him. In the painting *The Guilt of Gold Teeth* Jean-Michel had painted Baron Samedi, the chief of the Gede family of Iwa in Haitian Vodou, who received people into death and resurrection, in a top hat and long coat.

Suzanne had witnessed Jean-Michel practising Vodou spells at the MoMA by sprinkling water under works by Picasso, Van Gogh and Matisse. On his paintings Jean-Michel would write

'GOLD' or 'NOT FOR SALE', which were Vodou spells, as were his works on money.

When Suzanne's relationship with Jean-Michel was broken, painting became a way for her to feel close to him, and his work was mirrored in her work and themes. Painting was Suzanne's Vodou magic, a way to spell Jean-Michel back into her life. Even her work *In Memory of Joan* was a Vodou spell. Her large painting of Joan Burroughs is illustrated with a big red apple on Joan's head. She holds one hand up to her face as she looks at her husband, and the gun he is pointing straight at her, as she peers back at him through the scope of two fingers.

Jean-Michel introduced Suzanne to William Burroughs and they'd been to his readings. In Mexico, where I grew up, Burroughs was a legend. He'd killed his wife, Joan Vollmer, at the Bounty bar in the Roma neighbourhood of Mexico City playing William Tell.

In Mexico we knew that on 6 September 1951 Burroughs was so drunk he'd placed a highball glass on Joan's head and decided to show off his marksmanship. We knew Burroughs only drank Oso Negro gin with the little black plastic bears chained to the bottle.

A few witnesses who were at the bar confirmed to the police that Burroughs said, 'It's time for a William Tell act.'

His .38-calibre gun missed.

Later he said his gun 'shot low'.

While I wrote in my notebooks and Suzanne worked on this painting, we were reading Burroughs' books. Every now and again, Suzanne and I would stop and talk about many things but we were focused on Burroughs' ethical ideas on the danger of careless wishing. Burroughs wrote he would never be so stupid as to wish for money or wish for someone to die.

In the Mexican newspaper photos at the crime scene, the unbroken highball glass was on the ground beside Joan, who had been shot straight in the middle of her forehead. The gruesome picture of Joan on the slab in the morgue with her lipstick intact was known to almost everyone in Mexico and was all over the crime tabloids, the *nota roja*, as well as the police report, which was a publication everyone could read. Joan was twenty-eight years old. Burroughs spent only fourteen days in Mexico City's Lecumberri prison, where Leon Trotsky's killer, Jaime Ramón Mercader, was also being held. Joan Burroughs was buried in Mexico City's American Cemetery.

Burroughs and Basquiat belonged to the heroin aristocracy and Basquiat had painted references to Burroughs on one of his canvases. The bullet that killed Joan appears in Jean-Michel's triptych *Five Fish Species*. On the first of the three panels, in acrylic and oil stick, he wrote 'BURROUGH'S BULLET' twice, and scrawled 'MOTHERFUKN SKULLBONE' on the bottom. On a penny he scrawled the date '1951', which was the year that Joan was killed. The second panel is filled with hobo signs and references to New York City. In both the second and the third panel Basquiat painted the letter 'S' inside triangles, which represented houses. 'S' is for Suzanne. Jean-Michel said, 'Suzanne, you are my home.' The date '1951' is also scrawled on a penny in this last panel. In

Jean-Michel's painting there were no accidents: everything had meaning.

Slowly, over a year, as Suzanne painted her canvases, her streaks of messy red paint covered the floor and mixed with Basquiat's paint.

The floorboards became a palette of her colours and his.

Her green paint splattered over his gold paint.

His white paint disappeared under her yellow streaks.

Her red and his blue became violet.

On those floorboards, I walked over the paint ocean landscape called 'The End of Love'.

As a little girl, growing up in Mexico City, I knew the end of love was everywhere.

Mexico City

Some Facts

My parents moved to Mexico in 1960. My father was from New York City and my mother was from Nebraska. He was a chemical engineer who had been sent to Mexico to help build the country's first water treatment plants. My mother is a painter. When we moved to Mexico, I was a baby and my elder brother, George, was almost three years old. Two years later my sister, Barbara, was born.

My parents thought they would live in Mexico for a few years, but they would never leave and could never give a reason for this inability to depart. They sold their house in the United States and my father quit his job to make sure we would never go back.

The American Dream was a dream they never had.

Calle Palmas

Mexico City spread out across the valley under a sky of shoes.

In the 1960s, Mexico City was covered with electrical wires and tram cables so that a web of crisscrossed lines framed the clouds. Almost everywhere, pairs of shoes, tied together by their laces and tossed up in the air, dangled over the wires. The south of the city smelled like an open sewer because of the tall smoke-stack of the pulp paper mill, which let out plumes of dark-brown smoke. It was part of the landscape, like the volcanoes that surrounded the valley.

Women grew their hair down to their knees and sometimes sold it for braids, and many people were cross-eyed, as this condition could not yet be fixed at birth. Children had their heads shaved twice during their early childhood because, according to everyone, this would eventually lead to a full head of thick hair.

On Calle Palmas, in the San Ángel neighbourhood of Mexico City, there were wrought iron bars on all the windows. Every house was surrounded by a wall, which was lined with shards of glass made from broken bottles. The jagged and sharp blue, yellow and green glass spikes and splinters kept out thieves and, in the sunlight, the walls sparkled as if covered in jewels and crystals.

The evenings were skies of swallows and, once the sun had set, the garden lit up with fireflies. Every year on the festival of San Juan, on 23 June, after the first rains of the rainy season, the rooms of our house and the grass and trees in the garden would be covered with swarms of the chicatana flying ants.

Calle Palmas was filled with noise. It began very early with the first sounds of the street sweepers, with their brooms made from long, dry tree branches. The call of faraway roosters came in through the windows. Then, the whole day long, vendors with donkeys would come by selling wood for fireplaces or carrying fruit, brooms and clay pots. Every vendor had a whistle, a bell or a cry.

Bird sellers would bring canaries and parrots, which they carried on their backs in a tall stack of bird cages. Sometimes they even sold exotic birds from the jungles of Yucatán. You could hear the bird vendors from far away as they imitated the whistles of the birds they sold.

There were two ice-cream sellers who appeared on Sundays with a wooden cart pushed forward on wheels and bells attached to the handlebars. In the cart was a large wooden barrel with the ice cream inside, usually lime, mango or mamey flavour. The carts had names. One was called *La desgracia de Pearl Harbor* (The Misfortunes of Pearl Harbor) and the other was called *De todo los hijos de mi mama, yo soy el favorito* (Of all my mother's children, I am the favourite).

17

Frijol

My street was called Calle Palmas (although it is now called Calle Diego Rivera) because of the two large palm trees in front of my house, which framed a large black gate. This was topped by tiles, which formed a coat of arms with a yellow crown, shield, winged dog, tree and a wreath. These heraldic symbols were surrounded by sixteen tiles painted with the black figures of a man, a woman and a goat, and were as old as the founding of the Hacienda de Goicoechea on this land in 1776.

My house was two short blocks away from Frida Kahlo and Diego Rivera's studio. The muralist and architect Juan O'Gorman had built the house for Frida and Diego in 1931. It is known as the Studio House but everyone in the neighbourhood called it the Twin House. This was because there was one studio for Frida and another for Diego, joined by a small bridge, which was an expression of their autonomy and dependance.

Even though Frida and Diego had died some years before my family moved to this street, the Studio House still smelled of the painters' turpentine, oil paints and cigarettes. Diego's bronze death mask was on a small table and his studio was kept just as he'd left it. Even the seven or eight enormous Judas puppets made of papier-mâché stood against one window. His large shoes lined a wall and tables were covered with palettes and paint brushes. There were dozens of pre-Hispanic clay figures of people and dogs, and pots on many shelves; unfinished paintings rested against a wall. There was almost always a large glass vase filled with fresh calla lilies standing near his collection of leather and papier-mâché toads and frogs.

Next door lived the Borisov family, in a house that had once been Juan O'Gorman's studio. These two houses were the only modern, functional architecture buildings in a colonial neighbourhood with cobblestone streets. The Borisovs had moved to Mexico in 1948 to flee the second Red Scare.

Saul Borisov was a master weaver who was originally from Belarus. His work was curved, had slits or was completely crooked since he wanted his art to battle against the loom's symmetry. The walls of his house were hung with tapestries of huge orange suns, animals hiding behind weeds, fruit trees and bulls in bullrings covered with flowers.

The Lombardos lived a few blocks away and had four daughters. Dr Luis Lombardo was one of Mexico's most respected neurologists and one of my father's closest friends. He once went on a hunting trip and came back to Mexico City with a baby ocelot, as he'd killed the mother without realising there was a newborn kitten hidden under her body. The baby ocelot was named Frijol. When the feline became full-size, it was permanently locked up in one bedroom, which no one had the courage to enter because the ocelot was fierce. Even the maid refused to clean the room. Mrs Lombardo was the only one who dared to carefully open the door and take in the ocelot's food. Her arms and hands were covered with small bites, claw marks and deep scratches. These wounds were vivid purple from the gentian violet everyone used as an antiseptic. It was a kind of national uniform. The bodies of children recovering from chicken pox were covered in purple polka dots. Even animals were stained. White dogs turned violet and once I saw a donkey with a purple leg.

Frijol was given away to Mexico City's Chapultepec Zoo after Dr Lombardo realised his newborn baby girl could be prey for the wild cat. For many years afterwards, we would visit Frijol at the zoo.

The outside houses and streets remained the same while the inside of our house went through a metamorphosis.

My mother bought most of our furniture at the Mercado de la Lagunilla, which was also known as the thieves' market, from a man who had been a general during the Mexican Revolution. He was impeccably dressed in a clean brown shirt, brown trousers and riding boots and he had a large Zapata moustache. He told my mother he'd killed at least five people during the revolution. My father said that every man of a certain age in Mexico claimed to be a general in the revolution.

The general's stand inside the market had dusty antiques piled one on top of the other with no care for their value. He had a few chickens that lived inside one large white marble bathtub. He said the bathtub was an exact copy of Empress Carlota's bathtub that could be seen in Chapultepec Castle. The general had some chairs with lions carved on them that he insisted were from the time of the Vikings.

Our house in San Ángel slowly became filled with the general's antiques, and the sensible furniture, which had been brought from the United States, disappeared. A normal set of drawers was replaced by an eighteenth-century church cabinet that had been used for the altar cloths. The functional dining-room chairs were replaced by a set of twelve high-backed Austrian Gebrüder Thonet wicker chairs. The only room that remained untouched was the fourth bedroom, which my mother used as her studio, where she painted and sewed and made huge papier-mâché animals and cloth collages.

A Russian ballerina who lived in two rooms of a house behind our house and down a small alley also seemed to become part of our home's transformation. She walked around the neighbourhood throughout the day and was almost a beggar. Her clothes were in tatters but they were tatters of pearl-white silk stockings, crinolines, pink leotards, deep-green taffeta skirts and long tutus. Once in a while, she'd ring the doorbell and ask my mother for leftover fruit. She spoke only a little Spanish, and English with a strong Russian accent.

Nobody remembers her name. Some people said she was the ballerina known as 'The Russian' whom D. H. Lawrence had met at Lake Chapala, near the mining town of Ajijic, when he was writing *The Plumed Serpent*.

My drawers were filled with her ballet costumes, which she gave to me over the years and always came stuffed in pillowcases for

21

bags. I played in these tutus and dresses for years and her scent of Shalimar perfume permeated everything I owned.

The ballerina told me she'd met the great Anna Pavlova in 1919 when she came to Mexico on a dance tour. Pavlova had dressed as a China Poblana, which consisted of wearing a floor-length skirt decorated with sequins and Mexico's flag, with the eagle on a nopal cactus with a snake in its beak embroidered with red, white and blue thread. Pavlova had danced the *jarabe tapatio* on pointes for a crowd of 30,000 in Mexico City's main bull ring. When Pavlova finished her dance and fell into a deep curtsey, the crowd cried '*Ole!*' over and over again, as if she had been making veronica passes with a cape. The men in the crowd then threw their hats into the ring, as if Pavlova had danced among matadors and bulls on a ground covered with blood and fallen sequins.

What Was Given

Frida Kahlo liked to rest in bathtubs. At any lunch or dinner party, and after a few glasses of tequila, even though she preferred whisky, if possible, she'd go in search of the bathroom. Once there, she'd step into the waterless tub fully dressed in layers of skirts and petticoats and with her shoes on. Frida would sink down, as if the bathtub were a hospital bed or as if she were a mermaid in search of the sea, and rest her body.

Ruth, Diego's daughter, lived in the Studio House with her children, Ruth María and Pedro Diego.

Ruth María was my first friend and the Studio House was my second home.

At the Studio House, Ruth María and I left Diego's side of the house and always crossed the short bridge from Diego's roof to Frida's roof and down the precarious external stairs into her house, where we spent most of our time. From the bridge we could see out to Calle Altavista and the San Ángel neighbourhood and look down on the tall wall of organ cacti below us. From there we could see the snow-covered peaks of Popocatépetl and Iztaccíhuatl. We did not see the volcanoes; we saw the myth. Popocatépetl, a warrior, had come back from battle to find that his loved one, Iztaccíhuatl, had died. For ever after, he watched over her death sleep. They were our Romeo and Juliet.

Frida's house had a small bathroom on the second floor. On hot May days before the rainy season, when the air was reddish brown with dust, Ruth María and I liked to fill the bath, slip off our cotton summer dresses and white leather sandals and cool off in the tub. Sometimes we'd dump half a bottle of egg-yellow Vanart shampoo into the water to try to make a bubble bath. Ruth María would stand up in the water filled with the thick yellow liquid and kick and stomp to churn it up or would kneel down outside the tub and try to stir the soap into bubbles with her hands. It never worked. But the cool water felt good and together we learned how to blow bubbles underwater.

Ruth María and I did not know the bathtub did not hold only our small bodies.

We did not know that the tub, with its round overflow drain and white rubber plug attached by a fine chain, had contained Frida Kahlo's body too.

Frida painted herself there, resting in the water, with many objects and people floating on the water's surface. This is an oil painting dated 1938 and named *What the Water Gave Me*.

The water held a large seashell full of holes, which were bullet holes.

The water carried an island with a volcano, a dead woodpecker and an empty Mexican dress.

In the grey soapy water, there was a small skeleton resting on a hill.

The bathtub, which held our small bodies, still contained Frida.

Ruth María Alvarado Rivera

Ruth María found me like a forgotten sweet in her pocket. She found me like a dried flower pressed in an old book.

Ruth María would have protected me against a bully, a knife, a bullet or anything. When I was sick with asthma attacks, she was frightened and would bring me bouquets of flowers from the San Ángel flower market.

We held hands. She kissed the top of my head and carried me everywhere, as if I were a part of her body. Her brother, Pedro Diego, who was closer to my age, was quiet and filled with shadows. He read books all day long and had stacks of papers covered with his drawings.

We were all wary of Ruth María's stepfather, the painter Rafael Coronel, and if he was at the Studio House we did not want to be there and spent our time together in the street. Both Pedro Diego and Ruth María said they were mistreated and beaten with a belt and locked in the bathroom, where the cook would slip them tortillas under the door.

Coronel liked to touch my hair, which was an unruly white-blonde mess of curls and knots. I think it was because of my hair that he nicknamed me 'Hadita', the little fairy. He had a handsome and kind face with deep black eyes, which could suddenly turn violent with a sarcastic grimace or sneer.

Coronel had an enormous mask collection in a studio on Calle Altavista, a few doors down from the Studio House. To get to Coronel's mask studio, I had to walk past a house where there was a family who had had twelve daughters. Everyone said they were twelve ugly daughters.

At his studio, there was not a single space that was not covered by masks of all shapes and sizes. Even the bathroom and kitchen had masks on the walls, from floor to ceiling. There were skulls with red eyes, and faces with long beards made of hay. There were tigers and jaguars and mermaids and monsters with noses that were snakes. He had masks from every region of Mexico. There was one of a man with a fish tail coming out of his head and another of a human skull wearing a crown.

In my very first dream at around age six, or the first dream that I remember, I am walking through the house on Calle Palmas and the walls are covered with masks. In the dream, I am able to float up and see the masks that are high up near the ceiling. Because of this, for much of my childhood, I was sure that I could fly. I was unable to differentiate between the real and dream worlds and I knew exactly what flying felt like.

Ruth María and I spent Thursday afternoons with Apolinar the gardener, who had dark freckled skin and reddish black hair, and took care of the neighbourhood gardens. He carried a huge

27

pair of scissors wherever he went and used them to prune trees and to cut grass.

Apolinar took cuttings from one house and planted them in another. He dug up roots and cut slips out of one garden and replanted them into another neighbour's earth. In this way all our houses became connected through a lineage of roses and bougainvillea.

Once, when I was digging a grave for one of my rabbits among the rows of white and lavender snapdragon planted by Apolinar in our garden, I found the small clay head of an ancient Aztec goddess. She fit in my hand.

Apolinar had been a bullfighter and attended the first bullfight held to inaugurate Mexico City's monumental bullring, La Plaza de Toros, and the world's largest, in 1946. There he watched Manolete, the greatest bullfighter of all time he explained, perform in the ring. A year later, Manolete died from a goring by the Miura bull, Islero. Apolinar named his only son Islero.

Sometimes, Apolinar would roll up his trousers and show us the round, oyster-shell-coloured wounds in his legs from the days he'd been gored in the bullring.

Apolinar told us he liked to rebel against anything that wanted to take his life. He said nobody fights a bull to die but the beauty of the bullfight fiesta depends on how willing you are to die.

Clásica Flor de Naranja Aguas
de Colonia Sanborns

Sanborns' Clásica Flor de Naranja Aguas de Colonia was used by everyone. Before leaving for school, the soft scent of citrus was dabbed on to my arms and neck or sprinkled into my hairbrush and then brushed through my hair. Men used it as an aftershave and women sprinkled it on their clothes while ironing. In Acapulco, we also used it to keep away mosquitos.

Brujas and healers, who practised spiritual cleansings in their homes and markets, used the cologne to rid the air of evil thoughts and spirits. Sometimes they used it as if it were baptismal water by dabbing it on the foreheads of the people who came to be cured or soothed.

Ruth María had an empty bottle of this cologne that had also belonged to Frida, which she kept in a drawer in her bedroom. There were also some small black hairpins in a little cardboard box of the Rosita brand, which had belonged to Frida. On the box was written that the hairpins had a soft tip that would not scratch your scalp and were malleable enough not to break your teeth. I'd witnessed everyone open a hairpin with their teeth.

29

At Celia's beauty parlour, where my mother had her hair done, Celia's front teeth were broken sharp bits from opening hairpins.

Frida had badly chipped her front teeth on hairpins so two of them were fixed with gold. As this was not a very romantic story, Frida claimed a stranger on the street had punched her in the face and had broken the teeth. Frida never painted herself with a smile.

Everything Was
What It Was

In our neighbourhood you could walk twelve blocks and visit General Obregón's hand at Obregón's monument. During the revolution, in Obregón's battles against Pancho Villa in 1915, his right hand had been injured and then amputated. An enormous monument had been built to this hand, which had been kept in a glass jar of formaldehyde by the doctor who performed the surgery. The building was circular and the hand was displayed in the centre under a large spotlight. This was all that there was to look at. The hand was pasty white and veins and bones floated out of the severed wrist. If we had visitors from out of town, we took them to see the terrible hand as a rite of passage into Mexico.

Across the street from Obregón's monument was the Convento del Carmen, which was a grand colonial church and nunnery where we could visit the mummified remains of nuns. The nuns' faces with gaping mouths and sunken eyes were as familiar to me as the faces of my family.

The San Ángel market was three blocks from the convent and the place where my mother did most of our shopping. The

31

market sold everything from plastic buckets to dead and living chickens, jungle birds in cages, piñatas and piles of peanuts. Here there were beggars who moved around on handmade carts with wheels because they were missing a leg or both legs.

At the market there was an animal psychic called Hortensia, who could find lost animals. If someone lost their rooster, donkey, cat or dog, they'd go and see her. She could find the lost animals in her dreams. A friend of my mother who lost her dog went to see the psychic. The dog had been missing for days. During the first sessions, which were held in the market next to the stand that sold threads in all kinds of colours for embroidery, Hortensia only had dreams that the dog was sleeping in her arms and said that this did not count. It was when Hortensia finally had a dream that the dog was sleeping at the foot of her bed with a pig that she knew the dog was safe and would be found, which it was.

Everything was what it was.

A cross-eyed person was cross-eyed.

Mourning clothes were worn for at least a year and, in some cases, for a lifetime.

In many villages across Mexico there was a tradition at the festivals: the ugliest man in the village was the ugliest man in the village and he had to dance with the prettiest girl.

The streets were given names that spoke to what had happened there. Calzada del Hueso means Avenue of the Bone, Barranca del Muerto is Gulley of the Dead Man, Calle del Degollado means Street of the Beheaded and Cumbres de Maltrata Summits of Mistreatment.

In every Catholic church a carved image of Christ's full body was on display with the palms of his hands nailed into the cross. Blood-red paint oozed from these wounds and from the wounds around his head from the crown of thorns.

Everything was what it was.

Suffering and injustice were suffering and injustice.

Chona

For the first ten years of my life, Chona was my constant care-taker. She was tiny like a child and had black curly hair. She liked to look at herself in mirrors so she could inspect her two front teeth, one of which was completely surrounded in gold.

Chona also chewed gum, which was made from the sap of the chiclero or chicozapote tree she bought from vendors or farmers who came to the house a few times a month. They also sold pre-Hispanic artefacts and pottery wrapped in sarapes, which they dug up in their fields.

In his book *General History of the Things in New Spain*, friar Bernardino de Sahagún, who journeyed to Mexico in 1529, described women chewing gum or *tzictli*, the word for chewing gum in Nahuatl, and the strict rules as to when and how they were allowed to use it. He wrote the gum snapped in their mouths like castanets.

When Chona couldn't get the gum, she'd tear off a piece of paper or newspaper and chew on this for hours. I wanted to be like her and she wanted me to be like her, so I also chewed on little pieces of paper. Sometimes the ink, from chewing on a piece of newspaper or a corner torn from a page of a comic book, would turn our teeth a dark grey. Chona also told me that as a child she'd been so poor she'd learned to eat paper so she would not feel hungry.

On Saturdays or Sundays, Chona took me to Chapultepec Park. Here we were not interested in taking the small train which circled the park. We did not want to rent a boat on the small lake, or buy balloons or pink cotton candy. The place we went to was the House of Mirrors, which was right before the steep climb up to the castle in what used to be the guards' quarters under Emperor Maximilian.

All along the walls of the long room were about three dozen convex and concave mirrors. In the reflections, I could see my body deformed into many shapes and sizes.

The mirrors did not show the round blue-white scars all around my right ankle from stepping into a wasps' nest, which had fallen out of a tree in the woods outside Valle de Bravo.

The mirrors did not show the teeth marks in my right arm from the attack by the Borisovs' dog, nor the scar under my left eye where a snake had bitten my cheek.

In that hall of mirrors, I knew what was coming. I saw my little girl body turn into an old woman.

Chona didn't know how to read or write. She did not know how to hold a pencil and held it in her fist as if it were a tool to dig with or a knife for stabbing.

I learned to read for her. I learned to write for her.

Chona especially loved *fotonovelas*. They were sold at the newsstand next to comic books on *La Familia Burrón*, and the comics *Memín Pinguin* and *Kaliman*. The USA comics like *Tarzán*, *Tom and Jerry* and *Superman* were all translated into Spanish.

Over time, my reading became perfected by Chona's weekly purchase, for only one peso, of the *fotonovela Doctora Corazon*. These publications were printed on cheap brown paper and told stories through photographs and drawings. Many of the protagonists were famous actors.

The inside covers had an advice column where broken hearts could write to Doctora Corazón about their problems. This advice column was called 'The Clinic for Souls'. I read all these real stories to her.

The plot lines in *Doctora Corazon* invariably had long telephone scenes, which lasted for many pages in order to both take up space and create suspense. There are dialogues I still remember because they began in exactly the same way:
    'Hello.'
    'Hello.'
    'Hello.'
    'Where do you want to call?'
    'Where am I calling?'

The covers of *Doctora Corazon* showed anguished men and women with their mouths open in shock, tears streaming down their cheeks, or with an ominous, shadowy presence reflected in the pupils of the eyes. The stories inside were announced in bold letters: 'After Many Years He Has Once Again Begun to Trouble Me'; 'Cruel Betrayal'; 'They Forced Me to Marry Him Without Desire'; 'Justice Came by My Own Hand'; and 'The Dove of Solitude'.

In these pages I learned about impossible passions between men and women.

The ABC Hospital

My asthma attacks and time spent at the hospital began immediately on moving to Mexico City. During severe attacks, my
parents would drive me to the ABC hospital, which had been
built in 1923 and was a good distance from our home in San
Ángel. At the hospital I would be strapped to a bed, tied at my
ankles and wrists, and placed in a plastic barrier tent with cold
mist channelled through an ice machine. Two cannulas would
be placed in my nose to try and pump my lungs and give me
oxygen and an inhaled formulation of epinephrine. A sub-
cutaneous injection of adrenaline was administered every few
hours. My parents would peer in on me through the fogged
plastic tent.

At home, while I was recovering from these torturous days in
the hospital, Chona used Vicks VapoRub to try and help me
breathe. She would rub my chest and back with this combination of menthol and eucalyptus mixed into Vaseline. She
kneaded the soles of my feet with the ointment and then placed
my feet inside plastic bags. Chona also took me to the public
baths in San Ángel, near the market, for steam baths. In the
huge white-tiled room filled with clouds of steam, I'd listen to

the neighbourhood gossip. Although we went on the days for women, and most were very poor and this was the only place they could clean up, they all bathed modestly in their blue, yellow and pink slips and underwear, which became completely transparent when damp.

Throughout my childhood, in the darkness at two or three in the morning, I would hear the shrill sound of wheezing in my lungs. I'd stand up, get out of bed and go into my parents' room. I'd wake up my father by touching his arm. It was so hard to both breathe and speak with air that only flowed in and never out. The first time I saw a fish gasping on the deck of a boat with its mouth wide open, I knew that kind of dying.

Dandelions

I could count every crack in the sidewalk, and every tree root that broke through the cement.

I knew where the dandelions grew between the cobblestones.

I spent my childhood running away from home, which was the voyage around and around the block – sometimes for hours – still hearing my mother's words or feeling the spanks and slaps. In a letter to her parents, my mother quotes me. She wrote: 'At age 3 and a half Jennifer says, "If you give me more hits I'm going to get so nervous I'll go to another house."'

During those years, the shiny gold or blue or red paper stars from school, which had been glued to the centre of my forehead, could be found along the runaway-from-home path and scattered on the ground.

As I ran away, I wept with my mouth pressed tightly closed.

Chona had told me I must be careful never to swallow a fly.

Ballet

Holding my ballet shoes, Chona walked me the four blocks to classes that were given by Madame Bannister, who was a spiritualist. Ballet classes started when I was four years old. Madame Bannister came from a British family of mediums who had moved to Mexico in the late 1800s. She was even her own father's medium and at their house, which was actually a large compound of houses for the whole family between Calle Reforma and Calle Santisimo, a sanctuary had been built for the séances, which was next to the room where the ballet classes were held.

It was Madame Bannister who showed me the entrance to a tunnel in this room, which joined a labyrinth of tunnels. During the Mexican Revolution in the early 1900s, a network of underground tunnels was built in order to hide from the chaos and violence. Many houses in the San Ángel neighbourhood are joined underground by these passageways.

There was a pianist who played for the ballet class at a stand-up piano. He mostly played Chopin for exercises – *plier, étendre, relever, sauter, tourner, glisser* – and Tchaikovsky when we were allowed free movement.

41

At this age, with ghosts nearby, I learned a military language, the metronome mathematics of the beat, which was the sound of my body, the heart inside. These first steps were the beginning of a lifelong allegiance.

In dance there was a loneliness I belonged to as I became swan and swallow, tiger and deer. Above all, the discipline of a soldier overcame me and the wood floor, barres and mirrors were both lake and battlefield.

Encyclopedia

'When the encyclopedias get here' became a synonym for something that would never happen.

I was two years old when my father bought a complete set of the *Encyclopedia Britannica*. It took a year for these books to come to Mexico by boat from the UK. Then the set spent another two years in the customs offices in the port of Veracruz before they were sent to Mexico City by train. The encyclopedias took so long that the experience of waiting for something with great reverence became a part of our lives.

The encyclopedia arrived on 25 May 1965. At the same time as we looked at the books, my father had his transistor radio, which was his favourite object, turned on at full volume. He was listening to the fight between Muhammad Ali and Sonny Liston when Liston was knocked out in the first round by Ali's 'phantom punch'.

To the sound of the boxing match, I began to understand that the Nile was the longest river in the world and that the river was also in the word.

The word balloon was a balloon.

I Have Always Loved
Stories About Orphans

The fairy tales that were first told to me before I could read, the very first stories inside me, were filled with orphans. Little Red Riding Hood, Cinderella and Snow White were all alone. And, even before I learned about these stories, I knew Chona was an orphan. She told me her stories about her home at the base of the Popocatépetl volcano, where she and her sister grew up without their parents, who had died in a typhus epidemic.

Every twelfth of December Chona took me to give thanks and praise to the Virgin of Guadalupe at the basilica in Tepeyac, far from the neighbourhood where we lived. In the crowds from all over Mexico, I saw lepers with sores on their faces and growths on their hands and feet. There were children with terrible wounds and illnesses and some were carried on make-shift cloth stretchers. The blind were guided or walked tentatively alone with a long tree branch or broomstick for assistance. Most people were barefoot and there were many who moved along the dirty, crowded sidewalks and streets on their knees, which were wrapped in rags that bled through, while some walked with no protection and their knees were a blood-soaked mass of flesh and bone.

There were emaciated stray dogs everywhere in search of any scrap of food. Beggars lined the streets in rags and some sat on the floor holding out their cupped, wishing-well hands.

The roads were lined with trios and mariachi bands singing birthday wishes to the Virgin of Guadalupe. The lottery ticket vendors cried out that the Day of Guadalupe was the luckiest day of the year. People carried bags of confetti and threw fistfuls of it everywhere.

At the basilica we had to get into a long line and it took many hours of standing with the crowds in the sun before we could see the ancient fabric on which the Virgin of Guadalupe's image, surrounded in gold stars, was framed above the altar. Many years later, in 1979, when art historians studied digitised high-resolution images magnified 2,500 times, it was discovered that the Virgin's pupils held the miraculous image of an indigenous family made up of a woman, a man and three children along with other people, including Juan Diego, who witnessed the miracle of her appearance.

Chona had a small worn card of the Virgin of Guadalupe that she carried at all times. On the cardboard was written: 'Little Brown Virgin: Now that you performed the miracle of becoming an Indian, I beg of you to make us your children, brothers and sisters.'

Chona was deeply religious and, unbeknown to my parents, she had secretly taken me and my sister to be baptised by the priest at the Convento del Carmen. Barbara was a baby and so I was only about three years old. Many years later Chona confessed to my parents that she'd done this. She thought my parents would be angry but my agnostic father and mother thanked her for this act of love.

'We have a long way to go'

The postman came to our street twice a day on a bicycle. He would pick up letters to post and drop off letters that had arrived from around the world at the Palacio Postal of Mexico, which was downtown next to the Bellas Artes opera house. Letters used to arrive every day and my parents would write letters to their parents in New York and Nebraska twice a week.

I have boxes filled with the letters my parents wrote to my grandparents. As there were very few shops in Mexico City to buy clothes, almost everything was handmade. There are letters filled with swatches of cloth my mother included to show her parents the dresses she was making.

One letter from my father to my mother in the early 1960s when he was on a trip to Peru says, 'Break Jennifer's spirit before I get back home.'

To which my mother answered, 'I'd better go to bed right away and get some rest. We have a long way to go.'

In letter after letter my mother wrote to her parents, there's constant mention of my defiance against authority.

My mother said to me, 'You are destined for wonderful things or prison.'

I burned my left hand to the words, 'Do not touch the iron.'

Girls in Mexico had their ears pierced at birth and my parents thought it was barbaric. I was the only girl I knew who did not have pierced ears. I tried to pierce them all by myself when I was six years old with a sewing needle. The needle went straight through both earlobes.

I hated going to the doctor and so my mother had to lie to me and pretend we were going elsewhere. I would never open my mouth for the dentist. My mother had to find a dentist who was also a psychologist to try to coax me to open my mouth with games and rewards.

I did not like to eat anything that had colour. This was probably due to complications I had at birth which meant I didn't eat much as a newborn and had to have my stomach pumped and other procedures, which in those days were often done on newborns without anaesthesia. Chona became complicit in my tastes and would buy me bread rolls at the bakery, which I ate with butter or mayonnaise: white on white.

My mother bought all kinds of strange delicacies at the market for my brother to eat, as he enjoyed eating weird things. Once she bought frogs' legs for lunch, which I refused to eat. I kept my mouth tightly closed and ran away from the table. My mother followed me in a dash around the house with a fork raised in one hand, a piece of the frog's leg pierced onto the prongs. I ran toward the bathroom, but my mother was so fast. Growing up on a farm in Nebraska with three brothers, no one could beat her in a race. She could shoot a rifle, climb the tallest tree and steal birds' eggs, and she galloped the horses faster than anyone.

As I ran to the safety of the bathroom, my mother was able to wedge her foot in the door as I was desperately trying to close it. She then kicked the door open and pushed me down on the floor tiles and held me there with her knee pressing hard on my chest and the fork held above me like a dagger. I clenched my teeth together and never opened my mouth. She finally gave up, moved away and did not speak to me for days.

My mother told me that if I said dirty words, she was going to wash my mouth out with soap. At bathtime I would practise placing the soap inside my mouth so that when the time came, I'd be ready.

In one letter my mother wrote to her parents when I was eight years old, she says, 'Jennifer is a fearless swimmer – completely fearless. We can't glance away for a second.'

The Girl Guides was founded in Mexico in 1930. My mother thought it would be a good idea for me to be a part of this organisation, as it would straighten me out like a ruler.

Every Saturday I had to put on a uniform with a grey skirt, white shirt, knee-high socks, a kerchief around my neck and a short cape. We met in the garden of one of the guide leader's houses, where we marched and held up three fingers as part of the Guides pledge. We had to write down our daily good deeds in a notebook and read these out to the group. Small stacks of wood and twigs were set up along the garden's paths and we had to learn to light a fire with two matches. We had to work toward cloth badges of merit that would be sewn onto our sleeves.

At that time, I was the only girl in forty years to ever have been expelled from the Girl Guides in Mexico. The note to my mother explained that I was being asked to leave for insubordination, inciting revolt and smoking cigarettes. I was eleven years old.

The words 'do not' were words I could not live with.

She Taught Me to Be
Afraid of Everything

When Aurelia smiled you could only see a great mouth full of bright pink gums. She lived with us for four or five years, cleaning the house and helping my mother in the kitchen. Chona hated her.

Aurelia liked to pinch me and twist my flesh in her fingers like a screw. In Spanish this kind of pinch is called *pellizco de monja* (the pinch of a nun). She was good at hiding what she did, and carved a small piece of skin from Barbara's armpit with her fingernail. She taught me to be afraid of everything, but this school-of-life-by-Aurelia had the opposite effect and made me afraid of nothing at all.

Aurelia said bats came out at night and left their saliva all over the eucalyptus tree. She said if I touched the tree, I would die since it left the tree covered in rabies. I noticed that there were often dead birds at the base of the tree, as well as dead butterflies.

Sometimes I would sit in the half-dark of Aurelia's room and watch as she rubbed sliced limes all over her body to try to make her skin lighter. She never threw them out so there were brown used-up limes everywhere. She kept dried chicken wishbones and old rotting onions and radishes on her windowsill. Chona said she used them for witchery.

It was thanks to Aurelia that I learned about the world. She told me about incest, murder, suicide, and every other kind of crime imaginable. Aurelia liked to buy the weekly magazine *Alarma!*, which reported all the most gruesome crimes that had occurred in Mexico during the week, accompanied by savage, graphic photographs.

One edition had a series of photographs taken of a woman whose lover had sewn her eyes and mouth shut with a needle and thread.

The Water Diviner

I never knew my mother had had an accident, a scrape or a fall until I saw a bandage or a scab. She was stoic and never complained about anything. The pain in her world went inside and stayed there like gulping in a great sigh and never letting it go.

My mother grew up on a farm in Nebraska during the Great Depression. She told me and my siblings to look where we were going and be careful of stepping barefoot on a rusty nail because we could get tetanus. She warned us of this often. There were no rusty nails lying around in Mexico City. It was a farmgirl fear.

While my father came from a Jewish family with a belief in science, reason and tolerance steeped in Voltaire, my mother's family came from a background that sought freedom of thought and belief. School and knowledge were sacred to both of my parents. In 1879 the Nebraska homestead was built by my great-grandfather, Nathaniel G. Clement, who'd brought a library with him across the plains in horse-drawn wagons. This library was the only one in that part of the Midwest and was used by many. According to family lore, this included a visit by Mark Twain.

In the time of the homesteading, one great-aunt was scalped during an attack by one of the Indigenous tribes of the Great Plains and survived. In Mexico, in my mother's top dresser drawer, we had a yellow knitted cap in a plastic bag, like an ancient relic, which this aunt had worn for the rest of her life.

When my grandfather was fifty-four, he discovered he was a water diviner. He never witched a dry well and found over a thousand wells in the area, which changed the Nebraska landscape from brown to green. He never charged for witching and spent the rest of his life reading books on water divining in order to try and understand who he was.

When he and my grandmother came to visit us in Mexico for the first time, my parents took them to visit the Pyramid of the Moon and the Pyramid of the Sun in Teotihuacan, a place where thousands of people had once been sacrificed. After driving for two hours from our home and as we drove closer to the archaeological site, my grandfather began to feel a terrible weight press upon his body. He said he felt very heavy. When we arrived at the pyramids and he got out of the car, he fell to the ground. It was as if he was being pushed down by a great hand, he said. Even his face was pressed against the dirt and gravel of the visitors' parking area. There was nothing to do. We could not stay. He crawled back into the car on his hands and knees.

Buttons

My great-grandfather Cohn, who had immigrated to the United States in the late 1800s, had made a living by selling buttons from door to door in all seasons. My father took me, and it was just the two of us, to New York City at the age of five to meet him.

My grandfather told me that the buttons that sold best were made of leather or animal horn, for men's jackets. He'd also bought exotic buttons in Chinatown that were covered in beautiful coloured enamels or made from glass and mother of pearl. Once he even bought a set of golden brass buttons shaped like shoes from an Italian merchant.

When I got back from New York, I took my mother's button jars from her studio and opened them up on my bed. It was like spilling open a jar of candy. My mother kept buttons for her dressmaking and used them on a few of her collages made of cloth. She had large brass military buttons, yellow and blue glass buttons, tiny pearl buttons, and even buttons she had brought back from my parents' long trip to Japan. The Japanese buttons were covered in very fine flowers, with coral-coloured enamel, and there were a few delicate ones in the shape of fans, painted with a gold-yellow enamel. I had not known buttons were my heritage.

The Latest Fashion

In Mexico my mother immediately adopted the latest fashion, which was *makech* brooches pinned to sweaters or blouses. They were made from live jewelled beetles and created around an ancient legend that told the story of how a princess had been turned into a beetle.

My mother's *makech* was covered in green stones so it looked like it was made of jade. These beetles, an average of four centimetres long, were covered with semi-precious stones stuck onto their backs with a strong permanent glue. A gold chain, which was also glued to the *makech,* was used as a leash so that the beetle would not fly away or get lost.

When my mother's friends came over, I'd watch the jewelled beetles walk over the women's shoulders and breasts.

My mother kept her *makech* in a glass box in a dresser drawer, and years after the insect had died, it was still there beside her dark-blue-and-white rebozo.

Family Collage

The year Armando Manzanero won first place at the Festival de la Canción in Miami with the song 'Cuando Estoy Contigo', which played on the Mexican radio non-stop, my mother made a collage of the family.

She created it on purple velvet with different fabrics, including silk brocade, pieces of embroidered cotton, lace and gold military-style buttons. In the family portrait, I'm holding a very large pearly pink sequined butterfly as if it were a pet. My father, who at home always wore loose-fitting elegant kaftans of fine wool or cotton he'd have custom-made by a tailor, is wearing a kaftan with purple stripes as well as an Uzbek-style hat of black and white stripes. He is standing to one side of my mother and their three children. This collage is called 'La familia'.

My mother gave this collage to my father as a gift for Christmas. My father said we celebrated Christmas because we were agnostic Jews, Catholics, Anglicans, Buddhists and atheists. This was an identity he'd created for us.

Every Christmas Eve, my mother served us oyster soup, as this dish had been a tradition on her mother's side of the family. We would sit in the dining room, which had been set with silverware, fine Limoges plates and tall tapered candles burning in the centre of the table. With a white starched linen napkin on our laps, we would drink the creamy soup. My parents would drink champagne and my siblings and I would be allowed to have a taste or two of it from a spoon. Every year, in every bowl of oyster soup, there was a real pearl secretly placed in the light-brown liquid by my mother. I didn't like oyster soup so inside my specially made butter-and-cheese sandwich, I always found a pearl.

Acapulco

Acapulco smelled like a mixture of coconut oil, tamarind, fried red snapper in garlic, the Sanborns' orange-blossom cologne and Coppertone sunscreen.

In my teen years when I dreamed of running away from home, I was always headed to Acapulco, where the moon burns hotter than the sun. Women in Mexico know if you're going to Acapulco anything can happen, so make sure you pack a wedding dress.

In Acapulco the legend of the Elizabethan sailor Sir Francis Drake, also a dangerous pirate, was still known to everyone. If you misbehaved as a child you were told 'El Drake' was going to come and get you.

We used to go to Acapulco at least six to eight times a year. The drive, with soldiers stopping us at several checkpoints, took more than seven hours along a narrow one-lane highway. We always stopped in the town Iguala for ice cream at the only Dairy Queen in Mexico.

All along the drive from Chilpancingo to Acapulco men, women and children from the small communities along the way lined the highway selling green and brown iguanas, turtles and tropical birds with feathers of many colours. My father had to be careful not to run into cows or donkeys that might be standing in the middle of the road. Dead dogs that had been run over were everywhere and vultures circled high above them, black silhouettes in the blue sky.

We would stay at the Mirador Hotel overlooking the large bay or in palapas that were rented by the night right at the water's edge. There were droves of pigs roaming the beach and families gathered together to wash their clothes in the salty sea water. Vendors, dressed only in underwear, walked up and down the beach selling shells, coconuts and tamarind candies. As part of the time in Acapulco, we never missed going to Roqueta Island to see the famous donkey that drank beer.

My parents would go dancing at night, doing the twist at the Acapulco clubs. During the day we'd go out on glass-bottom boats or fishing for sailfish. I, along with my siblings, was tied to the boat with a thick wet rope as there were no life jackets. We would stand at a safe distance and watch as the thrashing, long, brilliant-blue iridescent sailfish turned a dull brown as it died, only a few seconds after being pulled out of the water. On one of these trips, while snorkelling, my father found a small, ancient gold crucifix from a pirate ship in the sand.

On 22 November 1963, my family was at the beach on Roqueta Island, across the bay from Caletilla Beach. We were huddled under a large palapa hunting for sharks' teeth in the sand and drinking coconut water through paper straws, striped red-and-white, from holes carved out of the top of large green coconuts. We heard some anguished cries and looked toward the dock to see a young fisherman dressed only in a pair of ragged trousers run down the beach toward us. He shouted something and, as he reached us, he tried desperately to catch his breath. '*Su presidente. Su presidente,*' he said over and over again. My parents quickly gathered up the beach bags, hats and towels. The fisherman ran to our side and helped us as we stumbled on the hot sand, running to the small dock and our rented glass-bottom boat.

As we crossed the bay back to Acapulco, we moved over the water where a bronze statue of the Virgin of the Sea was submerged under the waves. Through the glass in the bottom of the boat, we saw a halo of yellow fish swim in a circle around the Virgin's head.

When we reached the dock at Caletilla, Chona, who went on these trips to Acapulco with us, took Barbara, who was only an infant, back to the hotel. The rest of us went to our Peugeot, which was parked in front of the small hotel and had a radio.

My brother and I sat in the back seat with the car doors wide open. Our skin stuck to the red leather as we sweated in the humid, stifling-hot car. I kept very quiet as I watched my father pull up the car's long antenna and then sit inside adjusting the white knobs on the radio to find a station without static.

As my father had worked for JFK's presidential campaign and had been active in the civil rights movement, they had been invited to the Inaugural Ball in Washington, D.C. The day following the inaugural, my parents took a street sign that was being thrown away by the crew of cleaners. The sign said: 'NO PARKING JFK INAUGURAL'. It was packed up and brought to Mexico, where it stood behind my mother's row of shoes at the back of her closet for years. They were also invited to attend the ball for JFK when he visited Mexico in 1962.

My mother and father wept as we listened to the news of Kennedy's assassination. Their tears flowed out from under the rims of their dark Ray-Ban sunglasses onto their cheeks. I watched as the hope-birds flew out of their mouths.

The Parents Were Elsewhere

The twin sisters, Dominica and Marta, came from Oaxaca to work for us after Aurelia left. The twins could hardly speak Spanish. They were identical, with long black hair that grew down almost to their knees. They had a glass jar filled with small black-as-black stones and tiny pebbles from a comet that passed over the sky above their village.

The twins said that their dream in life was to visit María Sabina, who lived in Oaxaca and was considered Mexico's greatest healer. María Sabina was famous internationally and songs were written about her. It was well known that Bob Dylan, Timothy Leary and Carlos Castaneda had visited her in order to experience her 'mushroom evenings'. The twins wanted to eat María Sabina's mushrooms and see God.

Once, when they came back from the Easter holiday in Oaxaca where they had visited María Sabina, they were so excited they took me to their room and showed me a yellow rag that had mushrooms in it. Brown and grey, the mushrooms looked like small, meaty, wrinkled ears. The twins said that when they'd taken the mushrooms with María Sabina, they'd both become silver staircases.

One night when my parents had gone to a party, the twins said I could try one, but could only take a little bite because I was a child. I was seven years old, the exact age that María Sabina had first eaten mushrooms.

María Sabina recounted, when interviewed years later, how she came to take the mushrooms. One day when she and her younger sister were outside watching over the hens so they would not be taken by hawks or hungry foxes, they came across a small clearing with a growth of brown mushrooms. María Sabina said they played with the mushrooms at first as if they were strange little dolls and then ate them and saw visions. She explained that when they ate the mushrooms, both sisters miraculously stopped feeling hungry, which was all the time, and cold.

The twins took me into the kitchen and placed one mushroom on a plate and covered it with honey. They cut it up like a cake. I chewed the little mouse-sized piece Marta gave me and the twins finished the rest. I don't remember having a hallucination, but the twins said I became very quiet and didn't speak to them for an hour.

When Chona found out about this, she punched Dominica in the face. Chona's small fist went straight into Dominica's jaw. Chona told me never to tell my parents. After this, Chona gave my mother an ultimatum: either the twins left or she left. My mother fired the twins.

Shortly thereafter, in a letter my mother wrote to her parents, she wrote, 'Chona wants a vacation because she can't stand the looks and smiles from people on the street.' My mother thought this was completely reasonable and told her to go home and rest for a whole month.

My parents were elsewhere. My father travelled all the time for work to Peru, Costa Rica, Nicaragua and El Salvador. My mother worked with many charities and took art classes. She sang in a choir that visited government hospitals and orphanages several nights a month.

My mother co-founded Pro-Salud Maternal with Dr Edris Rice-Wray, who came to Mexico from Puerto Rico, where she'd headed groundbreaking work on the birth control pill. The organisation was disguised as a place of support for women's health, but was a kind of guerilla warfare combating the Catholic Church's doctrine against any form of birth control. The group of women would organise parties and balls as a front for their fundraising activities, which were headed by my mother. The artist Feliciano Béjar, who was a great supporter of the cause, made drawings for the invitations and posters. For one of these galas, called the Sea Monster Ball, my mother made papier-mâché puppets of fish, turquoise seahorses and one two-metre-tall purple octopus with long arms. My mother worked on these puppets with Gemma Taccogna, the Italian-born papier-mâché artist who'd moved to Mexico in 1954.

At another of these charity events, which was a masquerade party held at the Cosmopolitan Club, my mother went dressed as Ophelia, holding wilted flowers in a lace handkerchief. My father went as Hamlet, carrying a Day of the Dead sugar skull.

My parents were elsewhere but all the parents were elsewhere.

In Acapulco, Ana, who went to my kindergarten, drowned in a swimming pool.

Two nannies, who were sisters, also drowned together in an Acapulco swimming pool and no one was sure how this happened. The four-year-old girl they were meant to be keeping watch over also drowned.

In San Ángel one boy drowned in the garden pond and another drowned in a bathtub when someone left the child to answer the telephone.

Teatro Iris

On weekends my father would take us to the opera. The once majestic Teatro Iris smelled of urine and perfume. It was a burlesque theatre by night and rented out to the opera and for other productions on some days of the week and for Sunday matinees. As we listened to the music of Verdi's *Aida* or Puccini's *Madama Butterfly*, the smells of cigarette and cigar smoke from Saturday night's show still filled the air and the floors were filthy. The cleaning staff consisted of one old man who would silently be picking up trash or sweeping up with total indifference to the fact that the opera had already commenced. We even had to lift up our feet while he swept.

On Sundays we would often go to the Anglican church with my mother. My father never went to church or temple unless he had to for a bat mitzvah or wedding. My mother took us to church because she thought it was good for us. She said, 'If you don't believe in God, your responsibility is even greater.'

The words from the King James Bible entered me and were some of the earliest sounds I knew. I felt flame and beauty in the words. The sound and cadence of the psalms and the ritual words of the liturgy became a part of me. On these church mornings, I was given a parallel English to my English.

Blindfolded

The seamstress came to our house twice a week. She could hold at least two dozen straight pins and needles pressed tightly between her lips instead of using a pin cushion. This sight led me to have fairytale imaginings of her swallowing a pin as I watched her speak without moving her mouth, creating a Spanish of strange sounds.

My mother would oversee the seamstress, as she knew how to make everything. On the farm, my mother had learned to sew and, even as a teenager, could reproduce dresses she looked at in the Sears Roebuck catalogue. In Mexico for a party my mother made a costume of a red fox out of some furry fabric. She sewed a small square music box into the fox's tail, which she wound up and played at intervals during the party. The music box played Mexico's national anthem, as it was the only music box she could find in the shops downtown.

My mother liked to blindfold her daughters during these fittings so that the dresses would be a surprise. As this happened in the early evening when we were home from school and my father was back from work, he would keep us company.

In the darkness from the cloth covering my eyes and tied around my head, I sensed the different textures of fabric on my skin and felt the prick of a pin at my knee from an adjustment of the hem or the warm touch of fingers marking the place for buttons down the length of cloth on my back.

Most times my father would sit quietly or talk to the seamstress, as he was curious about the lives of others. At other times, however, he'd take this moment when his two daughters were both standing very still and blindfolded to recite poems or read something to us.

My father taught me a way of living in which literature and life reside together and are equally important. He was passionate about Shakespeare's works and knew many monologues and sonnets by heart. He could recite poetry and worked to memorise poems so that they would become a part of him. He was a chemical engineer and an excellent mathematician and invented machines that are registered at the United States Patent and Trademark Office.

My father was obsessed with Leo Tolstoy's *The Death of Ivan Ilyich*. He used to paraphrase the ending lines at Ivan Ilyich's deathbed – the questioning of the life lived – as a way of saying, 'Watch out, beware, what will you be asking yourself on that last day of days?' Or he'd recite the unforgettable line from the novella, which is, 'Ivan Ilyich's life had been most simple and most ordinary and therefore most terrible.'

My father was constantly getting into fistfights. He would actually punch people in the face, get up from a table so quickly his chair would fall away and onto the floor. He'd wipe away the blood with a white handkerchief he always carried in a pocket. He beat up our French tutor's husband, who was a well-known doctor, philanderer and very jealous husband, as the doctor had accused my father of seducing his wife.

Once, we went fishing on the lake in Valle de Bravo. My father made Barbara and me wait on the dock for hours so he could beat up a man who, speeding by in a motor boat, had ripped our fishing lines to shreds, leaving them floating on the water's surface. As it grew dark and cold on that Saturday evening, we waited for the fight. When the motorboat drew inland my father was ready, his fists clenched and held up like a boxer. His anger filled the whole world.

Once, at a formal Christmas dinner for twelve in Mexico City, a man at the table said something racist. My father was sitting across from me. I put down my fork. I stopped chewing and stilled my breath. I never knew how my father's streetfighter anger might storm.

My father placed his white linen napkin on the table. He pushed his seat away and slowly walked around to where I was sitting. Then he very gently cupped his hand around my elbow and, with this gesture, pulled me up from my seat. We walked out of the party without saying one word. The memory of that touch, his hand cupped around my elbow, is a birthmark.

His anger filled the world and his ability to elevate everything also filled the world. He once told me how in the 1940s he and a woman had waltzed down the very centre of Fifth Avenue at three in the morning. They'd waltzed from my grandparents' uptown apartment in front of the Metropolitan Museum of Art all the way to Washington Square Park – a waltz that lasted seventy-five blocks.

Stay Quiet

As soon as I learned how to write I began to compose poems. I had scraps in a pink ballet-shoe box, which smelled of new leather. From the age of six to ten, my father had his secretary type up the poems I wrote in a small three-ring binder. I'd give him my poems in my little-girl scrawl and my words, which rhymed perfectly, would come back in the evening transformed into typed elegance. It was my first book.

Some titles of these poems are: 'Stay Quiet', 'A Captain', 'Venice', 'The Word Moon Looks Like the Moon' and 'Carousel Horse'.

The poem 'Carousel Horse' was inspired by an antique blue-and-red wooden horse my mother bought at the thieves' market, and had once been on a merry-go-round. She had it installed on a pole in the breakfast room off the kitchen. Many afternoons, I rode the carousel horse away from my house to anywhere.

In the poem 'Stay Quiet', I write about the quiet of objects: 'the silence of the window, the silence of the tree'. In these early poems, I already knew there was no insignificant stone. Here I can also see my early and for-ever-after search for solitude, a sister to silence, which is not a lack inside myself but a lack of something outside.

As I shared a bedroom with Barbara, which George had to walk through to get to his room, I could never be alone. I used to build walls around my bed with my mother's canvases.

I once showed my father my name written over and over again within two lines in a school penmanship book.

'How is this my name? How is this me?' I asked him.

My father changed his name at sixteen, which meant he needed permission from his parents, after suffering antisemitic violence and perhaps a particular antisemitic incident in New York. He never told us what had happened, but it was something that he treated with vodka.

'You will never understand your name,' he answered.

The Legendary
Children's Parties

At the beginning of November, my mother held a party that
was a cross between a US Halloween celebration and Mexico's
Day of the Dead. She'd take my siblings and me to the Milpa
Alta cemetery in the morning to visit graves on the Day of the
Dead and then she held the children's party at dusk.

RECIPE FOR A DAY OF THE DEAD PARTY
BY KATHLEEN CLEMENT

Place children in a circle and blindfold them.

Explain that a corpse dug up from a graveyard
will be passed around from hand to hand.

Do not tell the children this secret information:

Peeled grapes are eyes.

Boiled spaghetti noodles are veins.

The brain is a cold octopus bought the day
before at the Mercado de La Viga.

The party favours consisted of carnival eggs filled with confetti, which then covered the garden with a magic carpet of coloured paper dots for months afterward. Little wooden boxes were given as gifts. When you opened the box a snake popped out like a jack-in-the-box and stabbed your finger with a tongue that was made from a small piece of wire. We were all given a sugar skull with our name written on it in sugar paste. As there is no Saint Jennifer, the market never sold a sugar skull with my name on it. Every year my mother had one made especially for me in the Mercado de San Ángel.

The sculptor Helen Escobedo played the part of a fortune teller. She dressed up in a long skirt, huge hoop earrings and a bandana tied around her head. A tent made of blankets was set up in the garden and each child could take turns hearing their fortune. Helen even had a globe, which she had a glassblower make for her. She saw amazing things inside the dark black-and-green glass.

Once, when I was over at Helen's house, the writer Juan Rulfo was there having coffee with her in the kitchen. As I walked in from the garden, Rulfo looked me up and down and didn't answer when I said good afternoon. He only nodded his head to my greeting as he continued to study me, taking in my blue eyes and blonde hair as he smoked a cigarette in and out, in and out.

For ten years, Rulfo had been an immigration agent and his job had been to seek out illegal aliens who were hiding in Mexico. After a moment, with irony and almost a smile, he asked if I was an illegal alien. He asked if I had immigration papers. I was only about eight years old and didn't really know what to answer and the question made me uneasy. He said it was a true shame to think I probably had papers, as he wanted me to be illegal. He explained to me and to Helen that, in all those years of spying, he'd never caught a single illegal alien and had remained in a state of permanent frustration that would be with him for the rest of his life.

Thereafter, whenever I'd see him, he'd ask if I was sure, really sure, I was in Mexico legally.

The Edron Academy

At the Edron Academy in San Ángel, a British school that followed a strict UK curriculum, all the students became British and, for many of us, the English language became our destiny. Instead of learning about Mexico, we learned about sheep shearing, old pence and new pence, weights in stones and lengths in feet. We studied Paterson and Macnaughton's *The Approach to Latin* and learned vowel 'quantities' and inflections by rote and studied the theories behind Celtic ruins.

One of the founders of the school, Edward Foulkes, who came to Mexico with the British Council, had been a teacher for so-called 'sub-normal' sons of coal miners in Wales and had been horrified by the physical brutality used by teachers against these boys. He wanted our school to be free of tension and a place where no child would ever be turned away. Because of this, the school, founded in 1963, was filled with children who had been expelled from all the other schools in Mexico City. One boy, who at age ten was already a practised arsonist, set fires with tree twigs and dry red bougainvillea flowers, as if making a campfire, in the school's bathrooms. Some of these children were expert thieves and so you knew not to take anything you really liked to school, as it would be stolen. There was a boy who had been expelled from twelve schools and he was only ten years old.

At recess there was always a football game going on. Football had been brought to Mexico in the early 1900s by the British Blackmore family, who were beer brewers from Devon. They had founded one of the first breweries in Mexico at the beginning of the 1800s. In the iconic photograph of Emiliano Zapata and Pancho Villa, taken by Agustín Victor Casasola in the National Palace in 1914, there is a Blackmore standing in the background, who was Villa's personal doctor. Many years later, I married into the Blackmore family.

Beginning in first grade, we studied Shakespeare or attended plays put on by the older students. At age six I played the part of the fairy Mustardseed in one of these school productions of *A Midsummer Night's Dream*. Fairy Mustardseed only has five lines, which I recited to myself for months:

And I.
Hail!
Mustardseed.
Ready.
What's your will?

In the Shadow of Shadows

Every now and again in the San Ángel neighbourhood, as if it were its very own island in the city, the outside chaos, dreadful poverty, beauty and terror came inside.

Once, a rabid dog came right up to the window where I sat watching the street. I saw the white saliva and its insane eyes – eyes out of a Goya painting, my mother said.

The phones would ring up and down the streets when a rabid dog had been seen. For days our parents made us stay homebound.

Every block had a nightwatchman who blew a whistle on the hour throughout the night so everyone inside their homes would know all was well. It became a comforting sound that accompanied our sleep and dreams. One of our night-watchmen, who we could never forget because he was so beloved but also because his name was Dante Ovidio Perez, had been knifed and killed after working in our neighbour-hood for years.

As I grew older, I knew the shadow in the shadows was the

terrible brutality of the police force. We knew there was theft, corruption, drug trafficking, the trafficking of women and girls, torture and murder. People disappeared.

We knew you should never show any affection in public or there could be consequences. You could get beaten up for kissing on a park bench, under a tree or in a car. The judicial police drove around in dark, unmarked Ford Falcons without licence plates looking for prey.

The most frightening word we knew was Lecumberri. This prison was most likely the worst place in the whole country and we knew this even before Arturo Ripstein in 1976 filmed his documentary *Lecumberri: El Palacio Negro*, in which he recorded the filthy common toilets, scenes of walls covered in blood and horrifying rooms for torture.

Blanca and Her Chicken

While our house was filled with world literature and books on art and philosophy, my parents were both readers of contemporary Mexican literature. Octavio Paz's *Labyrinth of Solitude* was given as a gift to anyone who came to visit Mexico from abroad. Paz, in this work, wrote that the American, from the USA, drinks to forget, while the Mexican drinks to confess. When my father drank, he both forgot and confessed. He would wake up early and make a morning orange juice with fresh-squeezed, almost red-coloured oranges from Veracruz. The glass was half full so it could be topped all the way up with vodka.

Among my father's friends was the journalist Alma Reed, with whom he founded the Mexico chapter of Democrats Abroad in 1964. Alma was famed for her outstanding reports on the story of Simon Ruiz, a seventeen-year-old Mexican who was wrongly accused of assassination in the USA and sentenced to death by hanging. Her work helped to support the law that made it illegal to execute prisoners under the age of eighteen. She was also known for her in-depth articles in the *New York Times* on the smuggling of Mexican pre-Hispanic artefacts to the USA for the Peabody Museum at Harvard, which were stolen out of Chichén Itzá's sacred cenote.

Alma, while on assignment for the *New York Times* in Mérida, fell in love with the governor of Yucatán, Felipe Carrillo Puerto. His efforts to reconcile the Yucatec Maya and the Mexican government after the Caste War were remarkable. Known as 'the Abraham Lincoln of Mexico', he gave his first speech as governor in the Maya language. While Alma Reed was back in San Francisco for a short trip to buy her wedding dress, Carrillo Puerto and his three brothers, who were not supporters of a rebellion against the President Álvaro Obregón, were executed by a firing squad of rebel army officers.

Governor Carrillo Puerto had had a song commissioned for Alma Reed, which my father loved, called 'La Peregrina'. At parties or restaurants my father would ask the mariachi bands or trios to play the song:

> Pilgrim, you've left your places, the fir trees
> and the snow, the pure snow . . .

When Alma Reed died in 1966 her remains were taken to Mérida, where she was laid to rest at the General Cemetery. A group of friends, including my father, contributed to buying the plot in front of the governor's tomb so she could be buried with her lover.

At this cemetery is a gravestone with a stone statue of a little girl called Blanca holding a chicken. When Blanca's pet chicken was killed for the family meal, she died from grief. The family decided to bury the child and chicken in the same grave.

1968

For everyone in Mexico the date 1968 is the sound of a bell of warning and a gunshot. It was the year of the government's massacre of students in Tlatelolco. It was also the sound of Angélica María on the radio singing 'Cuando Me Enamoro' and The Cowsills singing 'The Flower Girl'.

That year five young mountain climbers, who had gone to Puebla to climb La Malinche, decided to overnight in the village of San Miguel Canoa. The villagers, incited by a right-wing priest, believed the mountain climbers to be communists or thieves and lynched the innocent young men. Two of the group were killed, along with two villagers, and the three survivors were critically injured. Two weeks later the Tlatelolco massacre of more than four hundred students occurred, which overshadowed the events at Canoa.

In 1976, Felipe Cazals made a movie, shot as if it were a documentary, on the events and called *Canoa: A Shameful Memory*. When I saw the movie at the Centro Universitario Cultural (CUC), with an opening frame that says '*ESTO SI SUCEDIO*' (THIS DID HAPPEN), it seemed more real than reality in the way some dreams are more real than reality.

Throughout the hours that we sat and watched the movie, it was as if something we'd once had had left us. All that remained there, in that movie theatre, was a terrible silence that entered everyone in the audience and never left. I had to constantly close my eyes. I knew I was too young to be watching *Canoa* and I knew I would always be too young.

1968 was the year of the Olympics in Mexico. For many, the singing of the national anthem throughout the Olympic Games, after the massacre, was a dirge. For the Olympics, Mexico City was turned into a showplace for the world. Almost every country sent a sculpture to represent their nation, lining the main avenue to the Olympic stadium, village and swimming pool. We all noted that the sculpture from France looked like President Charles de Gaulle's nose.

At these Olympics, the African American athletes Tommie Smith and John Carlos wore black leather gloves and raised their fists to protest racial injustice while standing on the podium wearing their champion medals. They wore no shoes, only black socks, to represent the poverty of African Americans. Martin Luther King had been assassinated only a few months earlier.

In Mexico City on that day, after both athletes had been suspended from the US team and expelled from staying in the Olympic Village by the International Olympic Committee, Tommie Smith said, 'If I win, I am American, not a Black American. But if I did something bad, then they would say I am a Negro. We are Black and we are proud of being Black. Black America will understand what we did tonight.'

The defiance and bravery of these two athletes made an impression on everyone and was widely covered in the Mexican newspapers. The actions of these athletes were a reflection of the banners carried by students in the marches weeks before: 'We don't want the Olympics, we want a revolution!'

In 1983, José González González, the man who had been the bodyguard of Mexico City's chief of police, Arturo 'el Negro' Durazo, wrote a book on the brutality, corruption and constant fear of those years called *Lo negro del negro Durazo,* which became a bestseller. González even recounts Negro Durazo's brutal torture (by half-drowning and the use of a picana to deliver a high-voltage shock to the testicles) of Fidel Castro and Ernesto 'Che' Guevara at a clandestine prison in Mexico City in 1956.

Mexico was ruled by the Napoleonic Code. My father was told by many that if he ran over someone with his car, and the person was injured, to immediately back up and run over the person again until they were dead. After this, he should speed away and hide the car in the garage for a few months. This was a joke and not a joke.

The Mexican laws that made anyone offering assistance to a victim an accessory after the fact is an important part of Malcolm Lowry's plot in his novel *Under the Volcano.* A bloodied man is lying hurt on the road with a straw hat covering his face and no one can do anything to help: '"You can't touch him – it's the law," said the Consul sharply.'

More About 1968

1968 was also the year my father went on a trip to the Soviet Union. He explained that he was going on this trip to look for the family's Jewish roots, which were in Ukraine. His first stop along the route was in Moscow, where he met with the US ambassador at the US Embassy. The ambassador said they could not speak in the embassy, as the whole building was bugged. Because of this, the ambassador took him out for a walk in a park and told him to beware of women, or men if women seemed to have no luck, who might try and seduce him and compromise him in some way.

After the visit to Moscow and Leningrad, as it was called then, my father went to Odesa to try and find documents on our family, who had been killed in a well-poisoning pogrom. My great-grandfather Silberstein was the only survivor and fled, at age fourteen, to the US with fifteen dollars in his pocket – or was he fifteen with fourteen dollars in his pocket? Nobody can remember. His father had represented Odesa at Theodor Herzl's 1897 First Zionist Congress in Basel.

My father came back from this trip to the USSR with a samovar, which he carried on his lap all the way from Moscow to Mexico. He also came back with a passion for the poet Osip Mandelstam:

> I have studied the science of departures,
> in night's sorrows, when a woman lets down her hair.

My father's closest friend in Mexico was the journalist Cedric Belfrage, who had also visited the Soviet Union. Although we had gone to the Belfrages' house for many years, it was when my parents were eventually divorced in 1970 that the visits increased. We spent at least one weekend a month with my father at the Belfrages' house in Cuernavaca.

Cedric had fled to Mexico when he was deported from the United States after standing up to the House of Representatives' Un-American Activities Committee (HUAC) and the banning of the Communist Party. His home became the centre for many others who had fled, such as Dalton Trumbo, Albert Maltz and Herbert Lieberman, as well as a place where Mexican writers and artists met. Cedric is alluded to in Carlos Fuentes' novel *The Years with Laura Díaz*, where he describes this crowd and the home as 'an asylum for political convalescents'.

Cedric and my father would talk for hours about politics and play chess while they smoked cigarette after cigarette and drank vodka.

Barbara and I used to lie on a blanket in the large garden under the shade of a huge jacaranda tree. Mary, Cedric's wife, would bring us books to read and plates of sliced carrots and jicamas covered in lemon juice and salt. Sometimes the sculptor

Elizabeth Catlett, who was there all the time, would join us under the tree. She said, 'Little ladies, just so you know, take a nap whenever you can!'

Elizabeth Catlett was a sculptor and lithographer who was known for her works on the African American experience. She made sculptures of people such as Harriet Tubman and Malcolm X and of anonymous workers as well as sculptures of African American musicians. In 1962, she took Mexican citizenship. In the FBI's file on Catlett there is reference to her friendship with Cedric and Mary Belfrage and my dance teacher, Waldeen. Her life in Mexico is described in detail and includes her arrest there and her support for the 1963 March on Washington for Jobs and Freedom. She, my father and others raised money in Mexico, which they sent to the organisers of the march in Washington.

In 2015, Christopher Andrew, the Official Historian of MI5, claimed that his research proved Cedric Belfrage worked for the British Secret Intelligence Service (MI6) and described Belfrage as the 'sixth man' of the Cambridge Five spy ring. Later that year, the historian John Simkin provided additional information, which corrected this: Belfrage was working for British Security Co-ordination as a double agent, which is why he handed information to the Soviets.

And many years later, my friend, the writer Sara Gay Forden, who lived to one side of the Studio House and had played Hermia in the second production of *A Midsummer Night's Dream* I was in, in which I was Helena, would tell me her father, who was in Mexico under State Department cover, was actually working for the CIA.

In 1996, I took the US poet Yusef Komunyakaa to Cuernavaca to meet Elizabeth Catlett and, just before entering her house, as we stood outside the door ringing the doorbell, there was a strong earthquake. We held on to each other as the ground moved and shook. When Elizabeth opened the door, she said to Yusef, 'This is how Mexico welcomes you.'

1969

My father bought our first black-and-white television in the United States and brought it back to Mexico so we could watch the moon landing. On the night of 20 July, we were allowed to stay up late and watch the moonwalk narrated by Jacobo Zabludovsky, who, at 10.56 p.m., said in an almost tearful voice, 'He is stepping on the lunar surface . . . This is a lightning bolt that divides two epochs as if through the middle of an abyss . . . stop your watches for ever . . .'

We learned that President Gustavo Díaz Ordaz had given a message that had been left on the moon, along with messages from other leaders, in which he made the conquering of the moon analogous to the conquering of the Americas. Everyone thought this was the most ridiculous thing ever!

Two months later the astronauts came to Mexico City. It was their first visit since the moon landing and they were greeted at the airport with flowers and mariachis. My father took us to the parade in their honour on Avenida Reforma. The crowd was so immense, my father had to lift Barbara up onto his shoulders so she wouldn't get lost.

Now that we had a television, we mostly watched Mexican programmes but many of the television shows from the United States were dubbed into Spanish. Through *The Little Rascals*, *The Addams Family* and *The Flying Nun* the world of the United States came into our homes. The writer Álvaro Mutis, who moved to Mexico in the 1950s fleeing the Colombian dictatorship, was hired to do the dubbing of *The Untouchables* into Spanish.

Thanks to these US television shows, the carousel made of wooden horses painted blue, red and yellow in Chapultepec Park was soon replaced with the Jetsons' aero cars, with their transparent bubble tops.

From the moment we had a television, I watched soap operas. Starting in 1969, from Monday to Friday, Chona and I watched *Simplemente María* for two years. It seemed the whole country, and all of Latin America, came to a complete stop when this soap opera was broadcast. Because of this demand, it could be watched twice in one day – at two p.m. and seven p.m. If you didn't have a television, you'd go to someone else's house. *Simplemente María* was about a young woman who came to the city to work as a young maid and becomes pregnant by a rich, upper-class man. My novel *A True Story Based on Lies* is, in many ways, an homage to *Simplemente María*.

Music, especially from the United States, became a part of our lives. Barbara and I liked to sit in the secondhand white Peugeot 403 with red leather seats and listen to AM radio in the afternoon after school. The ashtray was full of our parents' cigarette butts and I used to take them out of the ashtray, pull them gently back into shape, and pretend to smoke and drive. We listened to rock in English on Radio 590. The radio announcer created competitions such as The Monkees against The Beatles or Creedence against The Beatles. One could call in to the station and vote for your favourite group.

Barbara and I could sit there for hours hoping to hear our favourite song, which was Henry Mancini's 'Love Theme From Romeo and Juliet'. We'd been to the Manacar movie house to see Franco Zeffirelli's *Romeo and Juliet* and learned the terrible lesson about the consequences of a single mistake. Maybe if we listened to that music for long enough, we could sing the tragedy out of our bodies.

Two Lost Friends

At first Ruth María's mother was absent most of the day at the Studio House because she was a renowned and successful architect who established Mexico's architectural school. And then she seemed to disappear completely, as she had to go to Houston for breast cancer treatments. Pedro Diego survived those years thanks to the company of his dog, Chucho, a frog that lived in a shallow wooden box under his bed and an iguana that he often carried to school hidden in a small suitcase. Ruth María spent her days with me.

Ruth María and Pedro Diego's mother died in 1969 at the age of forty-two.

Boxes and suitcases were packed up. Ruth María and Pedro Diego watched their mother's architectural drawings and papers burn up in a fire in a large metal container on the patio. The two children left the house, where their stepfather continued to reside, and went on to live a back-and-forth life between their biological father's home and homes of other family members.

The door of the Studio House closed.

I lost my friend. I lost Ruth María's tall tree shade. The afternoons were empty of her sorrow.

And More Things

After Frida's death Diego Rivera said, 'I had lost my beloved Frida forever. Too late now I realized that the most wonderful part of my life had been my love for Frida.'

We all wondered how he knew this so late and after so much life lived. And it made everyone wonder: do we also know everything too late?

Reading the Trees

As I grew older, I no longer ran away from home by going around and around the block. By the age of seven, I used to walk for many blocks as far as I dared from my front door. By the time I was eleven, I walked everywhere alone.

As I walked, I read the trees, which were parchments on love. On every tree, and carved deep into the bark with a knife or the edge of a key, were hearts with initials or names inside, dating as far back as 1919.

There was one tall ash tree that grew in front of the house where Rafael Coronel kept his mask collection. This tree had the opening line of a poem carved into the bark and spiralling all around the trunk. I had to circle the tree to read a fragment, like an ancient oracle, cut deeply with one of Jaime Sabines' poems: *Espero curarme de ti en unos días. Debo dejar de fumarte, de beberte, de pensarte. Es posible.* (I hope to cure myself of you in a few days. I need to stop smoking you, drinking you, thinking you. It's possible.)

The Parties Were Dangerous

The art studio was a sanctuary and it seemed every husband in Mexico was jealous of Frank.

Frank Gonzales was a Chicano painter and teacher from the United States who opened an art studio on a large property across from Sanborns San Ángel. Frank was tall, with kind brown eyes and long hair and a full beard.

Frank's studio was a large open space surrounded by a garden, with a loft area in the middle of the room where Frank had a bed, a desk and his record player. Here the sixties' Flower Power movement took place in Mexico City. After Woodstock, everyone said Frank's studio was the mini Woodstock.

In the morning, artists took classes there or worked on their pieces and in the afternoon the studio was open for workshops for children. I took puppet-making and clay-building classes. Frank said there were only two rules in his studio: you had to finish what you'd started and you had to clean up. He liked to say, as a kind of motto, 'You don't have to talk, being yourself is enough.'

100

The Beatles were always playing, along with Jimi Hendrix and Janis Joplin. If Marcos, Frank's son, was around, Jefferson Airplane's 'White Rabbit' played non-stop.

Every girl wanted to run to and run away from Marcos. He was a magnet for misbehaviour. I never looked into his eyes because I knew he would catch me.

In the overgrown garden, there was danger. The garden air was filled with marijuana smoke and, I found out later, there was a lot of tripping on acid too.

Marcos decided one day that my sister and I would be the gardeners. He said this as a ceremonial announcement. We agreed to this without question.

Whenever Barbara and I were at the studio, we had to sit beside him under a large pepper tree while he would take out a bundle of marijuana that was rolled up inside a newspaper. He'd lay the bundle across his lap and clean out the seeds and sticks from the stash. Barbara and I were then tasked with planting the tiny, greenish brown marijuana seeds all over. Over time we watched the plants sprout up among the purple snapdragons and the party confetti that forever dotted it in green, yellow and blue.

Strangers

My mother took people into our house off the street. In a letter to her parents, she writes about the two maids she hired to do our laundry who were sex workers. They had spent hours sitting under one of the palm trees outside our house, desperate for work. My mother's reasoning for hiring in the letter was, 'They are not the best-looking prostitutes ever to be seen.'

My mother's habit of taking in strangers was something that became even more pronounced after she and my father were divorced. One day, outside on the entrance steps of Sanborns San Ángel, my mother met a daughter and father from India who had come to Mexico for medical care. The daughter had amoebic cysts in her brain that were causing her to have seizures. The seizures and the treatments were causing her hair to turn grey, which was a great worry to her father, as he said that no one in India would ever want to marry his daughter. My mother took them to her car, brought them home and they lived with us for more than a year while the daughter had her treatments.

A carpenter once came to work for us to help my mother build frames and stretch her canvases and, in the first week, he complained of a terrible pain in his throat. My mother went to the market and bought a small flashlight. She then peered into his mouth, where she was able to see a piece of a wooden toothpick stuck in one tonsil. My mother paid for the delicate operation to have the toothpick removed. After this, he confessed to my mother he'd killed someone. He worked for her and lived with us on and off for a decade.

My mother also took in Helen Escobedo's daughter Andrea when she was only three or four years old and the same age as Barbara. This happened gradually, as Helen travelled so much and, even when in Mexico, was elsewhere. Andrea became another sister and slept with Barbara in Barbara's bed. She even called my mother 'Momma'.

All animals loved Andrea. If we went to the pet shop, the turtles would come out of their shells to look at her. In the garden, birds would fly near her and land on her shoulders or head, as if she were a statue of Saint Francis. Only Andrea could pet our vicious guinea pig. Street dogs followed her on our morning walk to school. One Sunday afternoon a flock of wild parrots crossed the sky above our garden. We all knew this was because Andrea was napping on a blanket on the grass where the avocado tree had once stood before it was felled by a snow storm in 1967. This was Mexico City's last snowfall. As it happened on Barbara's fourth birthday, for ever after 'Remember when it snowed . . .' was Barbara's refrain, as if that night the snow had fallen for her.

Chona Marries Fidel

Chona married the good-for-nothing, very handsome Fidel, who was always chewing on a thin tree stick and wishing it was a cigarette. My mother couldn't afford to have both of them work for us, so they went to work for Juan and Helen O'Gorman. Juan and Helen had been married and divorced three times. Frida and Diego had been married and divorced twice. These marriages and divorces fascinated me and kept me counting. The artist José Luis Cuevas, who liked to proclaim that for lovers he preferred married women best, actually married his second wife fifteen times in all kinds of ceremonies, including a Mayan celebration.

When Chona moved to the O'Gorman house, I watched her pack up all her things. She'd been with us for ten years and for all my life. I was losing my mother, best friend and even my alphabet. She was the only person in the world who needed me.

The O'Gormans lived in San Ángel, on Calle Jardin, a block from my house, which meant I could easily walk to visit Chona anytime I wanted. The O'Gormans took me in as part of the family and I could come and go as I pleased.

In the O'Gormans' garden, which was wild and overgrown with orchids attached to the trees by the gardener Apolinar, Chona comforted me and held me close when I told her my parents were getting divorced. She explained to me that my father had never recovered from his mother's death a year earlier. My father's loss of his mother, loss of her constant affection, left him permanently bereft, in search of her, and thereafter he always dressed in black even if he wore other colours.

Juan O'Gorman said, 'Mexico, for me, represents love and peace and everything that is magnificent and marvellous in the world.'

Many years later, in 1982, it was in this house that Juan committed suicide. My mother said that Juan liked to speculate on how he would kill himself and be absolutely sure that it would work. Nobody took this seriously.

Juan killed himself by hanging, gunshot and poison on a day when nobody was home.

My mother wrote a long poem dedicated to Juan's wife and her dear friend, Helen, called 'Painter's Sunset', about Juan's suicide, which begins:

Not in the hall
But hanging from his favorite tree
In the orchid garden.
Those parasites hung heavy in the morning blood
Red, lavender, delicate and pale green
As cyanide taste and strong . . .

The Parties of the
Empire of the Illusion

Next door to the O'Gorman house in San Ángel lived the painter Carlos Tejeda and his wife Mercedes. Carlos painted the portraits of most of Mexico's high society of the 1950s and '60s, as well as large landscapes of the Mexican countryside. They had a daughter, Silvia, who became my constant friend once Ruth María had left the Studio House after her mother's death.

The Tejeda house was dark and smelled strongly of petroleum wax, which was used to polish the black stone floors. To get to the large garden, I had to walk past the dining room where there was an enormous portrait Carlos had painted of Mercedes dressed in a deep-red velvet gown that looked as if it were lit by the flames of a fire. The image was a shrine to her. Their love affair was legendary and in her bedroom she had many shoe boxes filled with his love letters.

Mercedes, at age eighteen, had been married off to a much older, wealthy man who was her boss at the company that made Pomada La Campana. When Silvia asked her mother why she had married someone she didn't love, Mercedes answered, 'I never said yes, but I stopped saying no.'

As a married woman with a son, Mercedes met Carlos at the legendary parties held at the house of Federico Sánchez Fogarty, who looked like Salvador Dalí, with wide-open eyes and a long, thin moustache that grew away from his face like the antennae of an insect. These parties were called the 'Great Saturdays' and the 'Parties of the Third Empire' or the 'Parties of the Empire of the Illusion' and were even written about in news-papers by Salvador Novo, under the pseudonym Carmen Reyes. Sánchez Fogarty had all the hit records of the time and pretended to be an orchestra director as he faced the record player with a baton, which was one of José Clemente Orozco's paint brushes.

Mercedes told me that on the night she and Carlos met at a 'Party of the Empire of the Illusion', Carlos asked her to dance in a section of the house called 'The Sleeping Lagoon'. 'Tuxedo Junction' by the Glenn Miller Orchestra was playing on the record player. The dance between Mercedes and Carlos became so passionate, Mercedes' jealous husband strode over to the couple and broke up the dance. Mercedes told me her husband grabbed her wrist and, in an intense whisper like a slap, said to her, 'Stop it! Stop it! Stop it!'

Silvia, a child of this love story, was seven years older than me. She smiled as if she were born with a well of laughter inside and, even as a teenager, she had strong smile lines around her eyes. Silvia's dream of becoming a concert pianist came to an end when a car she was in was hit by the Cuernavaca train at the Las Flores junction. She survived the accident but her left hand was a broken, wingless sparrow never able to open again. For this reason, Silvia was an accomplice to my constant rebel-lion. She knew many trains were coming.

Silvia gave me cigarettes when I was eleven years old and pot to smoke when I was twelve and promised we would get some peyote soon, which never happened, but this promise was there as a constant dream. When I told her that, years before, two sisters from Oaxaca who had worked in our house had given me some hallucinogenic mushrooms to taste, Sylvia thought this was an important ritual initiation in my life.

Silvia loved my poetry and was my first reader. She even kept copies of my poems in the desk drawer of her bedroom. Every time we got together, she wanted me to bring her a new poem. It was almost a condition to see her.

Mercedes was a practising medium and would go to the séances at the Bannisters' house. It was Mercedes who told me about mediums, hypnosis and communicating with the world of spirits. The Surrealist artists Leonora Carrington and Remedios Varo had also been involved in these practices for a time, but Mercedes never stopped.

Silvia was not interested in her mother's obsession, but I liked to sit in the garden with Mercedes while she told me about the experiences she'd had during séances. While she spoke to me, we were constantly interrupted by her small army of gardeners who came and went. Mercedes worked as a landscaper and created some of Mexico City's most beautiful gardens and interior patios.

Mercedes and I became accomplices in the world of ghosts.

I was only twelve years old when I walked with Mercedes to the Bannister house, where I had taken my first ballet lessons, for a session. John Lovett, Britain's most important medium according to everyone in Mexico, was going to place me into a lucid hypnosis, Mercedes explained. He was a short, mild-mannered man dressed in a conservative grey suit and tie and looked like a banker or businessman. He was soft-spoken and gentle. When I walked into the room, he stood to greet me. As he took my hand, the first thing John Lovett said was that I was a writer.

Mercedes walked me back home through the streets of San Ángel. She held my hand in hers. 'Even if we don't believe any of this, we had a fun day, don't you think?' she said. And then she added, looking up at the pepper trees that grew along the cobblestoned streets and the bougainvillea vines and ivy that lined the houses, 'In this life you have to make everything up. That's the only way one can survive it all. Do you know what I mean?'

'Yes.' I answered. I'd already learned not to let reality get in the way.

Like a Bomb Leaving

My mother attended seminars given by Toby Joysmith, who was a painter, teacher and art critic, and an expert on Mexico's muralists. He was a follower of Peter D. Ouspensky and gave lectures on Ouspensky's philosophy. My mother attended these lectures, had read most of Ouspensky's books and had notebooks filled with some of his quotes along with her own sketches. One quote she repeated frequently was 'All true art is in fact nothing but an attempt to transmit the sensation of ecstasy.' In addition, my mother began to go to Silva Mind Control Sessions a few times a week and went to lectures given by Erich Fromm on freedom and belonging.

These influences, along with the time she spent at Frank's studio, were the beginning of my mother's shift and move away from my father, who was drinking more than ever. My parents were eventually divorced and my father moved out. Barbara remembers the vision of him leaving with his suits still on the coat hangers thrown over his shoulder. And, shortly thereafter, my brother was sent away to boarding school at the age of thirteen.

After my father left, there were no longer lottery tickets lying around the house. He liked to place the tickets as a surprise among the flowers inside the bouquets he bought for my mother.

After this conventional marriage was over, my mother made the decision to be a committed artist. She never had a job. She refused to give painting or drawing lessons. She refused to give English classes or help in the support of her children and anything we had was thanks to my father, whose situation was always unstable.

My mother never bought us clothes or shoes or anything at all and she lived only from the paintings she sold. This was a pact with herself of extraordinary dimensions. She moved into a house that was only half built and was almost uninhabitable, she didn't have a gas stove for years and used an electric frying pan to even boil her water for coffee or tea.

Even though this austerity surrounded her, she still went to the local junk yards in search of materials she could buy to slowly build her house. Influenced by the architect Manuel Parra, one of Mexico's sublime architects, who created a new vision by recycling pieces from demolished houses, she bought Italian marble floors from a bulldozed mansion on Avenida Insurgentes for the floor of her ruined house.

My sister and I were both awed and horrified by this decision as we ate old, black, bruised bananas and drank powdered milk, bought in large cans, mixed in a glass with water. The refrigerator was empty. We opened the large white door to a cold jar of peanut butter, Clemente Jacques strawberry jam and white

111

Bimbo bread and nothing else. My sister and I slept to the sound of her banging and hammering as she made her own wooden frames for the canvases after we'd gone to bed.

My mother painted all day long and into the night, as if she were making up for all the time lost or as if she were running for a train or running away from the farm in Nebraska into the shelter of a canvas. At an art show, she would be impeccably dressed but all day she'd have only eaten half of an apple and a bowl of corn flakes.

She painted the wildflowers she would find out in the country-side around the city and often on the old road to Cuernavaca. She painted cosmos alone in a field as well as paintings of weeds, grasses, magueys and *oceloxochitl*, known as tiger lily. She painted the plants she found in Mexico City's abandoned lots in search of the original flora in Mexico's valley, as well as reinterpreting ecstatic visions of bougainvillea vines and jacaranda trees.

My mother's recipe for a mix to make jacaranda blue:
  Blob of dioxazine purple
  Blob of deep violet
  Blob prism violet
  2 blobs ultramarine or bluer blob of Windsor blue (not neces-sarily Windsor Newton)
  Then white of various amounts possibly also mixed with gel medium.

At this time, my mother also became an accomplished photogra-pher so that she could not only paint the fields of Mexico's wildflowers in danger of extinction but also register the valley's flora in photographs.

As my mother was also a seamstress, she took her knowledge of sewing and embroidery to her art and stitched right on the canvas. Many of these works were inspired by fabric designs from Mexico, India and Africa and the tradition of quilt-making in the United States.

When my father moved out of the house, my mother wrote to her parents, 'It was a relief to have him walk out the door. Like a bomb leaving.'

The art came first and this ethic, more an ethic for passion than an ethic for work, was a lesson.

Almost a decade later, my mother was going to marry a man who was rich and had standing in the community. Two days before the wedding, with a large diamond on her finger, a string of Mikimoto pearls in her dresser drawer and a soft, pink silk dress hanging in her closet, my mother cancelled the ceremony.

Gene, the painter Gunther Gerzso's wife, called up my mother in a panic and said, 'Kathleen, you can't do this. All the preparations have been made!'

'Yes, I can,' my mother answered.

'No, you can't.'

'Oh, yes, I can.'

This went back and forth a few times until my mother finally said, 'I will never paint again!'

Later in the day, Gunther called my mother and said, 'Listen to me, don't let anyone try to change your mind. Don't marry him.'

My mother never looked back over her shoulder at that could-have-been life.

Mexico's IX General Census of the Nation 1970

QUESTIONNAIRE GIVEN TO THE PEOPLE:

Section on Shoes:

1. *Do you wear shoes?*

2. *Do you wear* huarache *sandals?*

3. *Are you always barefoot?*

Section on Food:

1. *What did you eat last week?*

2. *Do you eat meat?*

Section for Women from Age 12 Onwards:

How many births have you had where the baby lived?

A Midsummer Night's Dream

The Young Unicorns, an acting company for children, was founded in San Ángel in the late 1960s. In a complete production of *A Midsummer Night's Dream*, I played Helena when I was eleven and, at age nine, Barbara played Puck.

The words filled me up as I fell in love with the boy who played Demetrius and he loved me back.

We entered the language of grown-ups in the bodies of children.

I wrote him poems.

Decades later he told me that he'd burned my eleven-year-old inked words of you and me and love in a small garden fire of leaves and dry grass when the play was over and I no longer wanted to spend time with him.

I can still recite Helena's words by heart. Sometimes I say them aloud to myself the way a bride tries on her old wedding dress and pearls to see if she still feels new.

In Shakespeare's words for Helena, I was learning who I might be:

> Run when you will, the story shall be changed.
> Apollo flies, and Daphne holds the chase.
> The dove pursues the griffin; the mild hind
> Makes speed to catch the tiger – bootless speed,
> When cowardice pursues and valour flies.

Nothing Came In and
Nothing Went Out

Mexican socks were made with practically no elastic and so we had to keep up our socks by folding them over rubber bands we rolled up our calves to below our knees.

Everything in Mexico seemed to be secondhand and recycled. Up until the North American Free Trade Agreement in 1994, Mexico was mostly closed to trade from other countries. When people who had worked for a foreign company or at an embassy left, everyone tried to buy the things they sold or get the things they gave away. People would buy the secondhand cars and appliances even if very few things could be fixed, due to a lack of practical knowledge or because there were no replacement parts.

If someone was travelling to the United States, we had a shopping list. My mother asked for light bulbs since they burned out in one day. I asked for hair conditioner, which was marketed in the early 1970s and came in metallic tubes like paint. For the first time, I could brush out the nests of knots in my curly hair. Before this, I had to cut the knots out with scissors.

There were no designer products, televisions, stereos, or the latest toys. We depended on the smuggled items found in the Mercado de la Lagunilla or the kindness, or corruption, of a customs agent to bring things into the country. It was a gamble to see if a customs agent would stop you or let you in with illegal merchandise. What they confiscated was often sold on the black market. There were endless stories about rebuying something one had tried to bring into Mexico at a *fayuka* (contraband) market stand a few days later. Sometimes the customs agent even told you where you could go to buy back everything that had been confiscated.

After my father quit his job to stay in Mexico, he worked for a Swedish company and then, in 1970, with a bank loan and savings, he built a small factory that produced ferrules. In Mexico, the pencil ferrules, which are the metal piece that attach the pencil to the eraser, were so poorly made that they always became separated. School children had small coin purses in which they carried the short pink erasers so they wouldn't get lost. My father began to manufacture ferrules that worked and tightly held the pencil and eraser together. The ferrules were bright red, blue, silver and gold and we used to make strings of them to drape around the Christmas tree.

Shortly after the pencil companies made their first orders, my father received threats and warnings. At first these threats consisted of phone calls. Then orders for materials he needed wouldn't arrive or would be stolen from the trucks on the way to the factory. One day a bullet hole appeared, shot through his car above the right front tyre. Two days later there was another bullet, which we found lodged in the motor. I still have these two bullets.

And then, late on a Sunday night, at almost two in the morning, my father received an urgent call from the nightwatchman. By the time my father crossed the city, those who ran the pencil-ferrule monopoly in Mexico had burned my father's small factory to the ground. All that was left was a sea of blue, green, red, gold and silver molten metal.

Perhaps because he had worked for a Swedish company, or perhaps because of JFK, my father came into contact with the ideas of Dag Hammarskjöld, whom he admired greatly and whose book *Markings* he always had close by. Kennedy had said, after the death of Hammarskjöld in a plane crash, 'I realise now that in comparison to him, I am a small man. He was the greatest statesman of our century.'

After the factory burned down, my father quoted Hammarskjöld and said to his children, 'Never, for the sake of peace and quiet, deny your own experience or convictions.'

Pachita

The title of a poem written at age thirteen: 'I Don't Know Anything About Making Wishes'.

My English literature and French teacher at the Edron, Mrs Elisabeth Pardo, whom I called Madame Pardo, encouraged my writing and spent after-school hours going over my stories and poems. For more than two years, I'd go to her house and we'd sit in her kitchen drinking hot chocolate while she read my work.

Madame Pardo was unable to have children. Someone told her she should go and see Pachita. When she told me she was going alone, I offered to accompany her.

Pachita was a psychic surgeon and is considered one of Mexico's greatest shamans. She was born in 1900 and died in 1979. To explain her gift to the biographers and journalists who were studying her life, she said that she was orphaned at a young age and raised by a man of African descent called Charles, who taught her about medicinal plants and also showed her how to read the stars. She said the first experience she had with her powers was when she healed a sick elephant at a circus. In her early years, she'd enlisted in the ranks of Pancho Villa during the Mexican Revolution. She had worked in a cabaret, sold lottery tickets on the streets and had once worked as a singer on public buses.

In Pachita's trances, which allowed her to heal and operate, Pachita said she was possessed by the spirit of Cuauhtémoc. On Fridays in the Roma neighbourhood of Mexico, people would line up for hours to see her. There would be rich people, politicians and the poorest people in the country standing in line to wait for their turn. Her surgeries, which included organ removals or transplants, were always performed with the same kitchen knife that had a handle wrapped in black electrical tape. There were never any scars or wounds left in the place where the patient had been cut open.

Pachita's extraordinary gift was studied by many, including Jacobo Grinberg-Zylberbaum, a psychologist and one of Mexico's most important scientists, who mysteriously disappeared in 1994, Alejandro Jodorowsky, the avant-garde filmmaker who formed some of his own ideas on psychomagic based on his experiences, and the writer Carlos Castaneda.

We had to wait in line for more than two hours to even get into the waiting room. In the long queue, there were two young children in wheelchairs in front of us and an old man who was so emaciated he had to sit on the cold sidewalk as the line grew long behind us. There was even a long, black, shiny Cadillac driven by a chauffeur with a man lying down in the back seat. Everyone tried to see into the dark windows to see if it was a famous actor or a politician.

The waiting room was small, with a sofa on one side and a few fold-out card-table chairs. There was a door at the left where people went in to be cured. I watched as the two children who went in to see Pachita in wheelchairs walked out of the visit on their feet.

When it was my turn, my name was called by a very tall man with a bald head who was Pachita's son, Enrique. I went into a small dark kitchen that was lit by one candle. The room smelled strongly of a mix of orange cologne and the smoke of burning copal. Pachita was sitting on a stool next to the sink and, with her left arm outstretched, she leaned on a cane. She was old, with a full head of dry grey hair. In a strong masculine voice, she asked me what was wrong. I told her I was having trouble concentrating, as I thought this would be a good ailment to have if one wasn't actually sick. I didn't understand then that concentration is a kind of piety.

Pachita told me to walk toward her and had me stand in front of her. Then she rubbed my arms and neck with a white egg while she spoke in Nahuatl. Following this, she handed the white egg over to Enrique, who rubbed it over my back and down the front and backs of my legs. He broke the egg in a glass of water and held the glass up to the candle. The yellow yolk and egg white floated in the water like a sea medusa. As a cure to my problems of concentration, she told me to smoke at least five cigarettes a day.

It was midnight when we drove back to San Ángel in silence through the dark Mexico City streets, which had practically no lighting. When we got to my house, Madame Pardo parked the car at my black gate between the two palm trees and turned

123

off the motor. She said that Pachita had told her not to worry and not to wish for children, as she had five children in her womb. Pachita did know everything and was a great shaman. Madame Pardo had had five miscarriages.

A few years later, Barbara, all by herself when she was twelve years old, took my father in a taxi to the Roma neighbourhood to see Pachita. But even Pachita could not heal all the ailments that come from alcoholism.

The Santa Martha Prison

My father's girlfriend, Ann, who was a psychologist, gave free counselling to foreign women in Mexican prisons. Barbara, at age ten, and I, at age thirteen, would accompany Ann and my father on these visits to the women's jail, where we met foreign women prisoners who were mostly from the UK, USA and Canada.

When we arrived at the jail, we had to show ID and then we had to walk, one at a time, through a long, dark corridor where the walls were painted an oily brown. Then we were patted down in a small shower stall by a prison guard. The large three-layer chocolate cake we brought in for the prisoners every visit was stabbed several times with a knife or poked through with a wire coat hanger to make sure there was no contraband baked inside.

These women were in jail due to drug smuggling, except for one who had killed her Mexican lover. One British woman had tried to smuggle drugs hidden in the soles of her platform shoes. Barbara and I played the role of hostesses as we walked around the jail's visitors' area offering the prisoners and the guards pieces of cake.

Some rites of passage are only meaningful looking back. In 2012, I spent time in the women's prison Santa Martha Acatitla while I did research there for my novel *Prayers for the Stolen*, on the stealing of girls in the state of Guerrero. In my notes I wrote: 'Here tattoos of flowers smell like flowers.'

The Days of the
Shared Suitcase

After the divorce, my father often took us on weekends to Valle de Bravo, southwest of Mexico City, where he rented a small village house. On one of these trips, my father took Barbara and me to our first cockfight. Even though I had been taken to bullfights since I was a child, I'd never been to a cockfight. They were not illegal but attracted criminal gangs, as the betting on these fights was a good place to launder money.

The arena was a dusty, dirty lot on the outskirts of the village, with rusty fold-out chairs arranged in a circle and a few filthy stray dogs in a corner. To one side there was a square red freezer that contained Cokes. Beside the freezer was a table with three large bottles of rum. Many of the men were drinking brown, fizzy Cuba libres out of plastic party glasses.

First, the strong colourful birds were weighed in a dark corner and then they were brought into the middle of the makeshift ring. When they were thrown at each other to initiate the fight, I could see the sharp steel hooks lashed to the birds' spurs sparkle in the flurry of flying feathers.

Halfway through the fight, the birds vomited bile and could hardly hold up their heads. The one bird that was left alive, although punctured and mutilated, continued to peck at the feathered cadaver for a few minutes. Then it pulled itself out of the clearing, dragging its feathers while the metal hooks on his talons left a trail in the dirt. An emaciated stray dog, which had been watching from the side, rushed quickly forward and opened its large jaws and crushed the broken mess of feathers. Somebody said, '*Que facil es morir.*' (How easy it is to die.)

In these years in Valle de Bravo, I used to go to parties held at Barranca Fresca, John Finny's ranch. He was an Irishman who had moved to Mexico in 1968. Barranca Fresca was hard to get to, travelling rocky, unpaved roads, but once there one encountered a lush green valley surrounded by woodlands. Once a year John Finny would organise a medieval party with real jousts on horses, with lances made of broomsticks and teams that had their own heraldry sewn onto cloths that could be pinned on shirts. Barranca Fresca was the stage for many love affairs: as if entering into another time in history shook up everyone's kaleidoscope heart.

The meals were based on a medieval feast. There was a lamb or two that had been cooked in a pit in the ground for two days, as well as a pig roasting on a spit under an open fire.

There were shooting contests as well. At one party, the Defence Attaché of the British Embassy, in his role as self-appointed shooting competition supervisor, shot himself in the leg by accident.

In later years, it was Sue Chapman, a great horsewoman, singer and extraordinary beauty, who led the equestrian paper chase in the morning. Over decades, as the director of Anglo Arts, she created strong cultural bonds between the UK and Mexico.

At the ranch, my own kaleidoscope heart was shaken into blue and red glass flower-stars when I met Juan David. He was the son of Archibaldo Burns, who was known to be Mexico's most handsome man and allegedly had broken up the marriage of Octavio Paz and Elena Garro. Ana María, who was the wife of Ramón Xirau, the Catalan philosopher and poet, told me the story. Elena Garro had fallen in love with Archibaldo Burns and all because of a suitcase, as in those days everyone shared suitcases. Elena Garro wanted to borrow Ana María's suitcase, but she'd lent it to Archibaldo Burns and he had not yet returned it. Ana María sent Garro to Burns's house to pick up the communal suitcase and this was the end of two marriages.

Ana María also told me another story about Elena Garro's temper. Once, when she and her husband had a very bad fight with Elena, Elena had sent the 'whole works' over to Ana María's house in revenge and as an announcement of the end of their friendship. The 'whole works' from the Gayosso Funeral Home was the complete set-up for a private-domicile funeral wake. When Ana María arrived at her house after a day out, the living room had been set up with rows of small wicker chairs, two empty coffins and two large funeral wreaths.

Even though Elena, one of the great Mexican writers of the twentieth century, had left her marriage, she never recovered

129

from her love for Octavio Paz, which became an obsessive hatred. She said later in her life, 'I live against him . . . I had lovers against him, I wrote against him . . . everything I am is against him.'

'El Tiempo Que Te Quede Libre'

My mother had a love affair with the composer and film actor José Ángel Espinoza Aragón, known as Ferrusquilla, who wrote a song to my mother called 'El Tiempo Que Te Quede Libre', which has been recorded by many artists. Over a few months, while he was composing the lyric and melody, he used to call her up. I watched as she sat in her studio holding the telephone to her ear as he sang the song to her over the phone.

My asthma attacks ended when I was thirteen years old, thanks to Ferrusquilla. He told my mother about a healer near the Mercado de la Lagunilla, on Calle Guatemala behind the cathedral, who could cure asthma and had miraculously cured him of a perforated stomach ulcer.

My mother took me to see this healer, who had a large stand of herbs, barks and mushrooms and all kinds of grasses wrapped in string. For more than six months, three times a day, I had to drink teas of strange black barks and yellow leaves, which tasted acrid and poisonous. Every day the teas were boiled up on the stove and filled the house with a caustic smell. I carried

131

these potions with me to school and dance classes in large glass marmalade jars and they cured me.

Ferrusquilla's daughter, Angelica Aragón, became an actress and is one of Mexico's great beauties. As she was brilliant, her father was torn as to whether he should encourage her to be an actress or study medicine, the latter of which was her dream. This was so difficult for him and Angelica that my mother even wrote about this conflict in letters to her parents.

Angelica and I became friends and more like sisters. One of her first acting experiences was in Alejandro Jodorowsky's movie *The Holy Mountain*. She, along with a group of about twenty other adolescent girls playing the part of robots in a factory, were dressed in very revealing uniforms. They had to line up and kiss the boss, played by Juan Ferrara, as if the kiss itself were a punching-out time clock at the factory. In the film, among the young women there is a sense of competition as to who might end up with the boss. Today, Angelica is an outspoken advocate for the respectful portrayal of women in television and film.

In *The Holy Mountain* there is a scene that references the massacre of the students in 1968. Jodorowsky creates a moment where the students are lying on the ground bleeding birds that fly out of the gunshot wounds in their bodies. Ferrusquilla, who lived in Tlatelolco in an apartment over-looking the square where the massacre of students took place, told me he had had to stay locked inside for two days, as it was too dangerous to go out. A few days later, when he left his apartment and moved among the ghosts of the assassinated

132

students, he walked among rows and rows of single shoes, the pairs all lost, that the beggars were selling for cheap. Shoes like fallen birds.

Decades later, I was with the Canadian-USA poet Mark Strand at a literary festival in the port of Tampico. He told me that his original last name had been Stransky and that his family were Jews who came to the United States from Poland. He explained that his father's brother had left the US for Mexico at a young age, more than seventy years ago, and had never been heard from since.

'He was lost in Mexico,' Mark told me and said it was his life-long dream to come to Mexico and try and find his uncle.

Because of my friendship with Angelica Aragón, I knew her mother and knew her mother's last name was Stransky.

Angelica and Mark were first cousins.

Trotsky's Rabbits

Fanny del Rio, who became a writer and philosopher, wrote poetry and became my first friend to share my interest in politics, literature and philosophy. Fanny was named after her great-grandmother, who had come to Mexico from Italy and whom everyone thought looked just like the actress Silvana Mangano.

By the age of thirteen, Fanny and I would go to the Ágora coffee shop alone on foot or by tram on a regular basis. At this café, which was also a bookshop, one was allowed to read the books even if you didn't buy them. It was difficult to get books in Mexico and they were very expensive. At the Ágora we ordered coffee and read Karl Marx as we tried to understand the revolutions that were going on in Latin America. Our ambitious reading list, which we failed at, included Plato's *Republic*, Machiavelli's *The Prince* and Rousseau's *The Social Contract*.

In the late sixties and the seventies, we went to see films at the Centro Universitario Cultural (CUC) movie house. Here we saw our first films by Ingmar Bergman, Sergei Eisenstein, Juan Bustillo Oro, Pier Paolo Pasolini and Andrei Tarkovsky. The

CUC organised film cycles based on countries or filmmakers. There was nothing solemn about these evenings, as the regulation of age restrictions didn't exist in those days and so the CUC was filled with crying babies and children running around on a ground covered in popcorn and candy wrappers. My mother took pillows for Barbara, age seven, and me, ten, to sit on while we watched Bergman's *The Seventh Seal*. The images of the chess game on the beach live inside me as if it were a dream I myself had dreamed.

In 1949, Luis Buñuel renounced his Spanish citizenship and became a Mexican. He died in Mexico City in 1983. Barbara and I also went to see his movies at the CUC. In his film *The Phantom of Liberty*, which is a defence of the imagination and dreams, there is a scene where a man moves a perfectly centred clock on the mantelpiece to one side and says he is 'fed up with symmetry'. Barbara and I used this phrase non-stop, as if it were a revolutionary credo.

At the Edron we also had film premiers and talks, which were mostly given by the parents of the students. Diego Genovés' father, the anthropologist Santiago Genovés, who was the mastermind behind the 'The Peace Project', came to speak about his research. He was a charismatic and handsome Robinson Crusoe, who dazzled the girls as he spoke and showed slides in our school's fake Tudor library built with long beams of dark wood. His experiment consisted of taking ten people (four men and six women) from the Canary Islands to Mexico on a large raft in order to study the cause of violence in humans and, perhaps, learn to prevent it. In his talk, Genovés told us he was interested in the connection between violence and sexual attraction, which is why he had only picked attractive people for the one-hundred-and-one-day voyage! Only years later did we find out this experiment was also known as 'The Sex Raft'.

Sometimes there would be concerts. Our friend Ana Thiel's father came to play for us with his orchestra of sixteen accordion players.

At school, current events and the exploration of political ideologies were ever-present. There were students at school from Chile who had fled after the coup and suicide of Salvador Allende. We knew of the terror in Guatemala under the Arana presidency through a schoolfriend whose extended family had been 'disappeared'. Gabriel García Márquez's sons went to the Edron and they spoke of the violence in Colombia and also brought back stories about their trips to Cuba. Once, they recounted how they'd become acquainted with Fidel Castro's dairy cows, which Castro personally named. Thanks to them, we all listened to the revolutionary songs of Silvio Rodríguez.

In my own home we would get terrible news from our cousin, Marshall Meyer, who, from 1958 to 1984, was the lead rabbi in Argentina. The sober reports on Argentina's 'Dirty War' were a part of our daily lives and we feared for the safety of our family when he told us about the missing and the treatment of prisoners in the jails. His fear was so great, he had had to build up the walls around his house and buy trained attack dogs. Jacobo Timerman's book on the atrocities of the Argentine military, *Prisoner Without a Name, Cell Without a Number,* is dedicated to my cousin Marshall. Today there is a square named after my cousin in Buenos Aires.

As we followed the events in Argentina, we read Julio Cortázar, whom we knew had left Argentina in 1951 and lived in France. In those years his experimental novel *Hopscotch* was being read by everyone in Mexico. At one time I could even quote whole passages by heart: 'Only in dreams, in poetry, in play do we sometimes arrive at what we were before we became this thing that, who knows, we are.'

We were close to the children of the Spaniards who had fled the Spanish Civil War to Mexico, which received more than 25,000 refugees. We read Federico García Lorca and Luis Cernuda, who was exiled to Mexico and died in Mexico City in 1963. After Cernuda left Spain, it was said that he never unpacked his suitcase.

In addition to political awareness, my group of friends, which included the writer DBC Pierre, were influenced by Latin American ideas of artistic integrity. We believed that creating for a market or public was irreverent and could ruin an artist. Cortázar had said that success, especially in the United States, was the last thing an artist wanted because he felt the reason for writing was to counteract the propaganda of those in power. We believed that if a book sold more than twenty copies it must be terrible.

In 1975, Cortázar published a comic book in Mexico, which reflected on his ideas about art and capitalism and was an homage to the famous French comic *Fantômas*. It is also considered an important contribution to the tradition of serious comics, such as Art Spiegelman's *Maus*.

Cortázar's comic, *Fantômas Against the Multinational Vampires*, was about the disappearance of the world's greatest books and

137

libraries by capitalist forces working against culture and the imagination. Some of the writers who appear as characters in the comic include Octavio Paz and Susan Sontag, who is drawn in a hospital recovering from a terrorist attack. Cortázar himself is represented as a character.

The comic opens with Fantômas speaking to the Italian novelist Alberto Moravia on the telephone in Rome:

Fantômas: Alberto, how are you?

Alberto Moravia: Worried, Fantômas, as you can imagine and you don't know the worst of it. Fantômas, I've been threatened, 'If you write another book, you will die!' What do you think?

Fantômas: Do you suspect someone?

Alberto Moravia: I think it's a fascist plot but it's hard to say who leads it . . .

A few calls later, Fantômas phones Octavio Paz in Mexico City:

Fantômas: How are you, Octavio?

Octavio Paz: Not well at all, Fantômas. This world problem of the books has me depressed.

Fantômas: Are there many problems in Mexico?

Octavio Paz: You can't find a single work by Fuentes, Yáñes, Rulfo and Arreola!

Fantômas: What a disaster.

Octavio Paz: People are weeping in the streets.

When we skipped school, Fanny and I liked to go to Trotsky's house. It had already become a museum, but no one visited the place. It was rundown and had basically not changed at all

138

since Trotsky's assassination in 1940. The bedroom wall still had bullet holes in the plaster from the first failed assassination attempt.

In the second and successful attempt on his life, Trotsky had been killed with blows from an ice pick. Since that day, it seemed, only the blood had been cleaned up and even the large desk where this assassination had occurred was in total disarray and untouched. The desk calendar was frozen at 20 August 1940 next to his eyeglasses broken from the struggle, a letter opener, a magnifying glass and a seashell.

The journalist and author Elena Poniatowska told me that in 1960 she'd been to visit the muralist David Alfaro Siqueiros when he was at the Lecumberri prison. She did not expect to end up meeting Ramón Mercader, the man who assassinated Leon Trotsky. Without thinking, she said, she shook his hand and for ever after felt the shock of that quick and thoughtless handshake – her hand should have fallen off her body, she said.

Mercader was an electrical genius and could fix all the prisoners' radios and even small transistor radios, which were their only access to the outside world. Because of this, he was the most popular and powerful man in prison.

At Trotsky's house, Fanny and I would go out into the garden, which was overgrown with bougainvillea vines and many species of cacti, and lie on the grass and smoke cigarettes and read our poetry to each other.

Trotsky's ashes were buried in the garden with his wife, Natalia, under a small monument engraved with the Soviet hammer and sickle. Fanny and I knew that Frida and Trotsky had been lovers and we also knew that Frida had been falsely implicated in Trotsky's assassination and was jailed for two days and one night.

The garden had more than twenty wooden cages standing on tall supports and circled by wire mesh. These cages contained Trotsky's rabbits, or new generations born from his original rabbits.

Wande

Wande was the son of the Ethiopian ambassador to Mexico under Emperor Haile Selassie's government. Wande was tall and slim and had a short black afro that crowned his head. I was thirteen and he was seventeen and he chose me. He chose me like the best apple from the pile of apples.

At school we'd go into the green-tiled girls' bathroom and lock the door. There, we would climb into the bathtub, which was also green, our beautiful pea-green boat, and sit inside it and smoke cigarettes and pot and kiss. The smoke would rise and blow out the window above us and over the garden below, where we could hear the sounds of our classmates playing football.

Wande would say to me, 'I want to be on your time,' as if the wristwatch on my arm had more minutes than his. I only understood what this meant after he and his family left without saying goodbye to anyone. At the outset of the military coup Wande and his family left Mexico months before the emperor's death, which may have been an assassination. I never heard from Wande again.

Aline Davidoff Misrachi

If it is true that fate gives you three chances to meet your destiny, I was given three chances to find Aline.

Aline and I could never remember the date or year we first saw each other but it must have been at the start of the school year at the Edron in the early 1970s. We recognised each other like a swift, passing glance of oneself in a mirror.

Aline was small and delicate; later my nickname for her was Hermia. In *A Midsummer Night's Dream*, Helena says of Hermia, 'Though she be but little, she is fierce.' I also called her Thumbelina and imagined her in a pistachio shell for a boat and a matchbook for a bed.

Aline wore dresses from shops in Paris while I was in the clothes my mother had made for me by the seamstress. At age eleven, Aline wore Chanel to school and had a black Givenchy mini dress she wore all the time. Her black hair was perfectly combed while I had a wild head of curls I could not control. My father's nickname for me was Mad Meg of the Moor because of this.

(He told me that as a child and adolescent he used to sleep with a stocking on his head to try and control his curls.)

My cousin, John Meyer (Rabbi Marshall Meyer's brother), was the famous and successful clothes designer John Meyer of Norwich. Once, he gave me a paper dresses made by the Scott Paper Company, which came folded in a box as if they were Kleenex. I wore mine to school. It was a maxi dress, which was light blue and covered in dark-blue-and-pink circles and very go-go.

Aline walked over to me during recess and looked at the garment intensely. Then she said, 'That is a dress to wear when smoking cigarettes.' Forever after we were each other.

Stories About Rings

At Aline's house everything was a mixture of old Europe and contemporary Mexico. Aline's father, Leon Davidoff, had come from Danzig, but the family had originated from Lithuania, though were Russian in their customs. Leon came to Mexico in 1941 on the SS *Capitaine Paul Lemerle*, which carried more than three hundred refugees. On board were a number of artists and intellectuals, including André Breton, the painters Wilfredo Lam and André Masson, and Víctor Serge (the writer and Trotskyist who was assassinated in Mexico) and Claude Lévi-Strauss. In his book *Tristes Tropiques*, Lévi-Strauss describes his first contact with Breton, which began on this ship under crowded, inhumane conditions: 'A lasting friendship was about to develop between us . . . during that interminable voyage . . . we discussed the relationships between aesthetic beauty and absolute originality.'

Aline's father became a successful businessman who, throughout his whole life, supported the arts, cancer research and treatment, and a peaceful Israeli state. The extent of his charitable work was vast. I once asked him why he'd decided to give so much of his money to cancer research and he said, 'If you live long enough, almost everyone will get cancer.' I accompanied him several times to a retirement home he'd built in Cuernavaca. It had a small state-of-the-art medical clinic, Chagalls on the walls and a beauty parlour for the women.

Aline's mother was a Sephardic Jew whose family had come to Mexico from Monastir in 1917. Aline's grandfather was Alberto Misrachi, who had the famous bookshop Central de Publicaciones, which was also an art gallery. Located in downtown Mexico City in front of the Palacio de Bellas Artes, the place became the heart of the city for writers, musicians and artists. Don Alberto, as he was called, had what Salvador Novo described in one of his volumes on *Life in Mexico* as an 'explosive dynamism'. Don Alberto was the first to exhibit paintings in the windows that faced the street and soon was the first to show the work of José Clemente Orozco, Rufino Tamayo, Diego Rivera's very first watercolours, and works by Remedios Varo.

It was Aline's mother, Ruth, who told me that Frida's body was so broken she liked to get up from the lunch or dinner table and find a bathtub to lie inside. There she would serve Frida whisky, sit on the edge of the tub and listen to Frida's stories.

When Aline's grandmother, Anna Arouesty, came to Mexico, she had her long, full braid cut off. She kept it in a box for years until she gave it to Frida, as Frida wanted her hair to be fuller. Frida often wore that braid like a crown. Aline's grandmother assisted Frida in all of her operations and would drive Trotsky around Mexico City in a white Jaguar. Aline told me that her grandmother only wore the perfume Fleurs de Rocaille, which she sprayed generously on her neck and the inside of her wrists.

At Aline's house there was a huge portrait of Aline's mother painted by Diego Rivera. In the work, she is lying on a straw mat next to a huge Olmec head, wearing a simple golden cuff bracelet and a ring that belonged to Frida. Inscribed on the canvas are the words *'para la niña de mi niña'* (for the little girl of my little girl). Diego called Frida his *'niña'* and Frida called Ruth *'niña'*. When Frida died, it was the chauffeur, whom Frida nicknamed 'General Trastornos', who gave Diego the news and said, 'Sir, *la niña* Frida has died.'

Remembering the day of Frida's death, Diego wrote that she had given him a ring the night before to honour their twenty-fifth anniversary – even though there were still seventeen days to go for that celebration.

When Aline's mother was hospitalised at the ABC hospital shortly before her death, two of her rings were stolen. Aline was so distraught by this, I took off one of my rings and placed it on her finger then and there. I was challenging a miracle. Aline knew that this act was an evocation. We liked to talk about how in history and literature rings have always been given to create magic, seal alliances, make pacts, set friendships, express lovers' vows or as remembrance. We also knew that on the voyage from Europe to Mexico on the *Capitaine Paul Lemerle* ship, Aline's father had hidden the family rings, their only valuables, inside a small clothes iron.

I did not yet know about Alejandro Jodorowsky's ideas on psychomagic and what he called the transformative power of shamanic psychotherapy. He had studied Mexican folk healers and had spent a lot of time with Pachita. When I did read Jodorowsky's book many years later, I felt a kinship to these ideas of directing the unconscious, or directing life, through words, objects and especially through unexpected acts that might challenge a miracle, like my mother placing a pearl in my sandwich or my father hiding lottery tickets inside the bouquets of roses.

At one time, Aline, the granddaughter of Alberto Misrachi, was engaged to my childhood friend Pedro Diego Alvarado Rivera, the grandson of Diego Rivera. The engagement was broken off and they never married. Many years later, Aline gave my daughter the engagement ring Pedro Diego had given to her, saying, 'This is a ring for you. I want you to have it so someone will remember that Pedro Diego and I loved each other.'

When I asked Pedro Diego about this ring, he said he bought it for Aline on a trip to New York.

After my divorce, I carried my wedding ring in my wallet for over a year, nestled between my credit card and driver's licence. I wanted to give it away to another woman, as a kind of spell to change my luck: to challenge a miracle. At Parque Mexico in the Condesa neighbourhood, I gave it to an Indigenous woman from Oaxaca who was covered in plastic and fake jewellery and who was selling chewing gum from a small box she carried in one hand. When I took out the ring and said it was for her, she placed it on her finger. She knew this day was coming. It was a duel with fate.

A diamond engagement ring that was given to me by a boyfriend in New York, I gave to the printer in downtown Mexico City to pay for my first book of poems. I did not sell the ring and I did not give the printer cash. I gave him the ring – and all the promises.

'¿*Oye, como se dice* window *en inglés?*'

The comedian Tin-Tan is said to have kissed more actresses than any other film star ever. The list includes Rosita Quintana, from Luis Buñuel's *Susana*; Amalia Aguilar, the Cuban vedette; Meche Barba, the rumba dancer; Tongolele and Silvia Pinal, among many others.

Tin-Tan was supposed to be on the front cover of The Beatles' *Sgt. Pepper's Lonely Hearts Club Band* album. As he was filming, he couldn't attend the photo shoot, but he asked Ringo Starr to place a drawing of Mexico's 'Tree of Life' in his place. Ringo agreed. Of course, everyone in Mexico knows and accepts this might have been one of Tin-Tan's many made-up stories, which doesn't even matter. It's true to all of us in Mexico.

Tin-Tan was famous for his extraordinarily brilliant code-switching and wordplay and great humour. '¿*Oye, como se dice* window *en inglés?*'

When Tin-Tan died in Mexico City on 29 June 1973, everyone in Mexico was in mourning. Barbara and I sat on the floor, crouched in front of the television throughout that night watching the movies *Calabacitas tiernas* and *La marca del zorrillo*, in which he played both father and son, and his most iconic, *El rey del barrio*. That night we ate two whole bags of Lágrimitas, our favourite candy. Lágrimitas were 'tiny tears' of sugar that were crunchy on the outside and broke in your mouth with a liquid burst of anise.

Barbara and I spoke, and continue to speak to this day, our very own secret codeswitching language. We knew that *aguas fiestas* were not water parties and that *mala leche* was not bad milk. We knew that there were whole worlds and concepts that did not exist in English. *Transnochar* (staying up all night) and *pena ajena* (feeling shame for the actions of others) and a *tuerto* (only seeing with one eye) and on and on. In Spanish the name Barbara also means barbarian, and this alone gave us an endless amount of word games and rhymes. Our mix of Spanish and English is our best language.

We knew that English words had no gender and that no one in English knew that a chair was a girl and that a desk was a boy. Decades later I wrote a poem called 'Making Love in Spanish', in which the objects in the room make love with one another, as well as poems on the Spanish and English languages and in which they sometimes appear as empires in conflict:

How should I walk among twenty-nine letters
of the Spanish alphabet
between the pillars a, b, c,
among the tombstones of R and P
and where the letter ñ has a halo?

To Walk Alone

To walk alone was to walk alone.

By the age of seven, I was walking alone to school, ballet class and the houses of friends. I was also running away.

As I changed from a girl into a woman, I constantly had my breasts grabbed and often, as a man walked toward me, he'd reach out with both of his hands to touch both of my breasts. On these walks I was grabbed by men on the street, my hair was pulled, I encountered exhibitionists, and once a man tried to push me into his car.

Standing on a tram, holding on to a strap, I would have to move away from the feeling of someone placing their hands between my legs.

Once, sitting in a bus, a man behind me took a strand of my long hair and began to suck on it. I didn't even know this was happening until a woman on the bus, who sat across from me, gave me a desperate look. I didn't say a word and just moved away to another seat.

In crowded places such as markets or squares, men would get too close and whisper disgusting words into my ear.

I never thought to be angry or violent or speak out. I never felt it was something I could fight against. It was to be endured.

This constant touching, as if I didn't belong to myself and my body was for others, was normal.

Today Mexico City has pink subway cars and pink public transport buses that are only for women.

Waldeen and 'The Dance of the Disinherited'

I had never stopped taking ballet classes and living deeply in the sea of my body. When, at age twelve, I began to study modern dance with Waldeen, my love of dance became an even stronger passion, dance combined with intellectual ideas and study. At age thirteen, I was the youngest dancer to audition and be accepted into her dance company.

Waldeen, who appears in the FBI files on Elizabeth Catlett as part of the group of US citizens working in Mexico for the civil rights movement in the USA, came to Mexico at twenty-five and introduced modern dance to the country. Everyone thought she'd been Diego Rivera's lover and he wrote an extraordinary tribute to the way she created a modern dance that was completely Mexican. She was a very close friend of Pablo Neruda, who'd moved to Mexico in 1940 and worked at the Chilean Embassy. She was Neruda's first translator into English.

Waldeen's greatest work was her dance La Coronela, which she choreographed to music by Silvestre Revueltas. The wardrobe and the masks were made by Germán and Lola Cueto. The work was based on the famous etchings by José Guadalupe

Posada of skeletons and skulls and divided into four episodes: 'Young Ladies of Those Times', 'The Dance of the Disinherited', 'The Nightmare of Mister Ferruco' and 'The Final Judgement'. The dance was performed with thousands of dancers in the main squares in villages all over Mexico. Waldeen called these public dances her 'mass ballets'.

Waldeen said La Coronela came to her on the New York City subway when she returned on a trip in 1939. Suddenly she thought of José Guadalupe Posada's lithographs as the foundation of a ballet and right there, in the dark underground tunnels of New York, she could see the disinherited with their rebozos and everything. She told me this to explain how mysterious creation can be.

Regarding her love for Mexico, Waldeen said, 'In Mexico there are many elements which can be used for movement and for technique. There's a whole physiognomy, a way of moving in Mexican life that is different from the way most people move in the United States. I think that there's a kind of sensuality that might come into the technique that I never saw in Martha Graham because she didn't have it . . . because she lived in New York.'

In 1973, Waldeen founded the Ometeotl Workshop, which was both a choreography workshop and a dance company. With this new company, she left behind her dances that praised the Mexico of José Guadalupe Posada with the dancing skeletons and the themes on the Mexican Revolution, and moved into Mexico's pre-Hispanic past. Waldeen asked me to join this new company and I danced with her for the next five years. Technique classes and rehearsals were held four times a week in the gym space at the Edron and at a studio she had on Calle Gelati.

I was the only dancer in the company who wrote poetry, and since Waldeen also wrote poetry, she and I would read our work to each other. In these times when were alone, she taught me that an artist needed to be socially committed but never dogmatic.

One of the dancers in the company was Claudia Salas Portugal, the daughter of the photographer Armando Salas Portugal. At her father's Bucareli studio, Claudia and I would sit at the dining-room table drinking coffee and reading books on pre-Hispanic Mexico from her father's library. These books allowed us to find images and ideas about the cosmos and movements, which we then used to create our dances with Waldeen. In the library there were reproductions of some of the Codexes, which we copied out on white drawing paper. For our dances, we created costumes based on some of the images we found in these books. We even made headdresses for our dances that were made from corn, corn cobs, seeds and feathers.

In these years, apart from working in collaboration with the architect Luis Barragán and taking extraordinary photographs of Mexico's many landscapes, Claudia's father took photographs of his thoughts. These secret experiments involved the projection of the images or impressions in his mind onto virgin plates, which were then developed into photographs. These ideas emerged from his readings on Theodore Judd Serios, who created 'thoughtographs' on Polaroid film, as well as the work of Joseph Banks Rhine, who founded parapsychology as a branch of psychology and who experimented with ESP research.

As extraordinary visons appeared on the virgin plates, Salas Portugal experimented with projections by moving further and further away from the plate until he was practically on the other side of Mexico City. The results were so remarkable even the parapsychology division of NASA dedicated to the study of paranormal phenomena became interested in this work and studied his experiments at their headquarters in the USA.

When I was sixteen, Salas Portugal hired me to translate some of his texts into English. He wrote poetry and kept careful logs, worthy of great explorers, on all his expeditions throughout Mexico. I worked on the texts he wrote on Mexico's canyons. I translated and typed:

> Dragonfly and violet, cascade and forest, crag and petal.
> Within an unknown scale of values, all things are
>   sensitive to light, to life and to God.
> Even rocks elevate their supplications.

Waldeen told me how she'd once been given a pair of Pavlova's pointes and had burned them in the garden when she gave up ballet for modern dance. She said that after she read Isadora Duncan's autobiography all she could think about was dancing barefoot.

Waldeen also expected each dancer to create her own dances through a process linked to ideas from Gestalt psychology and Carl Jung. Waldeen believed in Jung's theories on the Collective Unconscious and she asked that we try and find primordial movements and ideas within ourselves that were automatically universal. She said we should not look for artifice created for entertainment, but for an organic expression of human life.

The second time Aline and I found each other was with Waldeen. Aline had studied ballet and had dropped out of school in order to study dance in London and later in Paris. Aline was Waldeen's soloist and the dancer Waldeen loved most. Aline was very flexible and had a beautiful pointe. She danced with great passion. As Aline was constantly moving back and forth between Mexico City and Europe, she came and went in the dance company too, but her status in the company never changed.

On her first years in Mexico, Waldeen said, 'Everything was opening up for Mexican artists and they just carried me with them. They were my teachers – they introduced me to Mexico. They took me all over the country. We didn't have cars, so we took buses, trains, rode on horseback. We went to marvelous fiestas out in the countryside. I danced barefoot in the dirt. I was simply saturated with Mexico. I didn't want to go back to the United States . . . I remember walking down the street and trying to see how people walked so I could incorporate that into my dance. I remember that everything I saw went into the dance I was creating.'

The Days of the
Peppermint Frappé

As soon as Aline was in Mexico, she would call me up and we would spend as much time together as possible before she went back to Paris. During those years, we talked about Antonin Artaud, who had lived in Mexico, and his ideas on art and theatre. We went to every production by Alejandro Jodorowsky, who had transformed Mexican theatre through his ideas of freedom and through his Panic Movement, which was defined by terror, humour and euphoria. We knew we were the daughters of Surrealism and could quote the manifesto in defence of freedom in art written in 1938 by Diego Rivera and André Breton with the line, 'True art is unable not to be revolutionary'. We understood that Surrealism was not an art movement but a way of life and a mixture of the unconscious and conscious. Poetry was not an instrument of political propaganda but a revolutionary act in and of itself.

Aline and I created a dance based on André Breton's poem 'Sunflower', which is in his book *Amour fou* (*Mad Love*).

We drew the dance on paper and imagined two dancers as statues, based on Giacometti's sculptures, who come to life and dance on tiptoe surrounded by Chinese lanterns. We called the dance 'The Ball of the Innocents' after a line in the poem:

Le bal des innocents battait son plein
Les lampions prenaient feu lentement dans les
    marronniers . . .

The Ball of the Innocents was in full swing
The lanterns were slowly catching fire in the chestnut
    trees . . .

Aline and I understood that Surrealism was against 'miserabilism' and that it was filled with joy and poetry. In *Mad Love* Breton wrote that the movement itself was 'the dazzling revenge' of the imagination. The effect of these ideas influenced my books on the trafficking of girls in Mexico and gun violence. In writing on 'miserable' subjects, I searched for a kind of poetic enchantment as well as incorporating Breton's ideas of rational and irrational love.

Though we were steeped in Surrealism as defined by Breton, we accepted all other versions. We knew Borges felt the term should be Supra Realism and that Alejo Carpentier felt that the term was a European exotic vision of Latin America. Carpentier wrote that Europeans tried to create or impose the magic, which included fabricating it, so it was innately false. Instead, Carpentier said it was something inherent in Latin America and should be called the Marvellous Real, as it is in a 'raw state, latent and omnipresent'. Octavio Paz called Surrealism a spiritual movement. He said that apart from it being a school of poetry or art, its essence was the unity of art, poetry and a moral vision of the world. (Paz did not mean moral in terms of good or bad, but moral in the sense of a kind of integrity in one's work and life.) My preference was the Marvellous Real, but I changed it into The Marvellous Real and Terror.

Some nights I'd go to Aline's house, where there was always a party. Aline once said, 'If you think about it, these are the days of the peppermint frappé.' Peppermint frappé was a drink that her mother was famous for. The cool, bright, emerald cocktail was an homage to Carlos Saura's 1967 movie *Peppermint Frappé* about a man who pursues his brother's wife.

At one of these parties Edward James, the British poet and Surrealist, arrived with his two enormous pet iguanas on leashes. Ruth's great friend Bertha 'La Chaneca' Maldonado was always at these parties. La Chaneca helped the García Márquez family when they moved to Mexico and even provided the table where some of *One Hundred Years of Solitude* was written. She was a gifted translator and translated the movie *My Fair Lady*, along with all the complex lyrics of the songs, into Spanish. It is a tour de force. Whenever we were together, we'd sing out 'With A Little Bit Of Luck' or 'Just You Wait' in both Spanish and English versions.

I once noted to Aline that the painter Francisco Toledo never came to the parties. Aline answered, 'Francisco Toledo has not really touched the Mexico City social scene – only erotically.' It was well known that the Oaxacan artist had run off with Bona, who had been André Pieyre de Mandiargues' wife and, during her Mexican excursions, had become Octavio Paz's mistress. When Toledo stole Bona away, Paz never forgave him. Paz asked Aline's mother to promise she would never buy a painting by Toledo, which, of course, was a promise she did not keep.

Aline and I shared our love for poetry and we especially liked to read the seventeenth-century poet Sor Juana Inés de la Cruz and discuss her ideas against hope. Sor Juana wrote two sonnets in which she expresses the way in which hope keeps us from reality and is even an 'assassin' of reality. Hope, the poet explains, is really cruelty in disguise.

Aline and I kept the 'against hope' watch over each other.

As friends, we also shared a fear of the tsetse fly. The Mexican newspapers were full of alarming stories about an invasion of the tsetse fly from Africa. It was reported that a bite from the fly would give a person a sleeping sickness. Aline and I imagined ourselves living a Sleeping Beauty life.

Aline knew *Hamlet* by heart and in the early 1980s she even staged the play at a theatre in Cuernavaca.

If we were out in her parents' garden at night, she'd point up at the moon, 'Look, the moist star!'

Driving home from a party, she'd say, 'Well, it was all accidental judgements, casual slaughters.'

Aline always thought her mother and Octavio Paz had been in love and that her mother was one of the women who appeared in Paz's long poem 'Sunstone', one of the most important poems of the twentieth century. I told her she had to find out. Years later she wrote me this email:

161

From: Aline Davidoff
Date: May 8, 2008 at 10:59:02 AM EDT
Subject: notes on Paz

Dear Jen,
I didn't call you back because I had breakfast with my
mother and actually got her to spill some beans.
Octavio beans.

(How disrespectful it sounds, does it not, to speak so
of the poet?)

But. My mother declared that:

She was in love with him. He was in love with her.

That very often the motorcycle from Foreign Affairs
would arrive at that house in San Jeronimo where I lived
the first year of my life, with letters from OP to her,
letters full of passion and desire that she would burn
after reading them, so that no trace would remain. That
he was gorgeous and the relationship remained platonic.

That he asked her to go with him to India. That they
both cried at the café when she told him she couldn't.

That they exchanged souvenirs (*remembrances
d'amour*): she gave him a gold coin that hung from her
wrist, and he a 'corny' little porcelain box.

That they wrote to each other during those years in
India. That she only kept one of those letters . . .

A

The Decision of the Flower

In 1976, at sixteen, with much effort and sacrifice by my father, I left Mexico City and went to Cranbrook Kingswood boarding school in the US, which is part of the Cranbrook Academy of Art. This was a school that centred education around the arts. I wanted to combine my education with the study of dance, as I wanted to go to NYU's dance department and become a professional dancer. At Cranbrook I joined the dance troupe and also worked in the ceramics studio. In the first poems I wrote there, I describe my experience of working with clay: 'I hold sunlight and time in my hands.'

The first person I met was Beverly Brown, who would become a lifelong friend. She was African American, with light skin and cheekbones so high she had deep hollows beneath them. Beverly looked like the sister to Thutmose's bust of Nefertiti. She had a sharp jawline and a very long dancer's neck. Beverly was Mary Hickson's niece. Mary was one of Martha Graham's soloists. Beverly's beauty was in Mary too. When I met Beverly's mother and Mary's sister, Betty, the same beauty was in all three.

Beverly came from what she calls a very American African-American family of lawyers, teachers, doctors, artists and especially social activists. The importance of oral history and the search for family stories is a constant, and the poet James Ruggia, who would marry Beverly more than a decade later, calls this family characteristic 'ancestor worship'. Miranda, Cordelia, Julia, Sophia and Sarah, who had nine children with her enslaver who later moved them all North to live as a family, are mythical women to me.

Beverly was also a member of the school's dance company. We choreographed many dances, including a fervent dance to Stevie Wonder's 'Sir Duke'. *Songs In The Key Of Life* was all we listened to that year. The music seemed like an explosion within us. Sometimes our dance company was transported in a school bus to Detroit, as we were invited to dance at the Detroit public elementary schools for audiences of over seven hundred students.

Our fathers had both worked in the civil rights movement and they were both brilliant men – and alcoholics. Once, when my father came to visit me, Beverly and I organised a dinner for our fathers. Happiness and brotherhood fell upon the dinner table when both men ordered double vodkas.

In the decision of the flower, Beverly was the 'she-loves-me' petal on the 'I love you, I love you not, I love you, I love you not' daisy game.

That same year, before I left for boarding school, there was a literary scandal in Mexico. Mario Vargas Llosa punched Gabriel García Márquez in the face in Mexico City at Bellas Artes on

12 February during a private showing of the movie *Survive!*, a Mexican production about the 1972 air crash in the Andes after which the survivors had to resort to cannibalism. García Márquez fell to the ground with a bloody nose and blackened eye, which Elena Poniatowska treated with a frozen steak she ran off to find from some restaurant close by. Those were the days of treating black eyes with frozen steaks. The incident was all over the newspapers, but at school we never asked Rodrigo or Gonzalo, García Márquez's boys, about the incident and they never mentioned it either. At that time, I never could have imagined that decades later, when I was president of International PEN, I would have a public clash with Vargas Llosa after I visited two writers who were jailed in Barcelona.

Irene de Bohus

One summer, when I was seventeen and home from boarding school, I worked as a model for Irene de Bohus, who was known for her impressionistic portraits. I used to take a bus to her studio in her large house in the Polanco neighbourhood. When I arrived, I'd wait for her in the majestic, marble-floored entrance and she would then come down an enormous stairway to greet me. She came down step by step, holding the white wrought-iron banister as if she were a queen. Her face was flushed, as she had long baths every morning, which made her smell like gardenias from the Jontue soap she had in every bathroom. She was an old woman in those days and held her head high and was perfectly made-up and coiffed, as she lived by a standard.

Irene said, 'The minute this stops, the minute you stop having a standard, you're looking into the grave. Vanity is also life. You must have clean and well-kept fingernails for example. And clean teeth.'

Irene was from Hungary and close to Frida. Frida even painted Irene's name in big letters above her bed in the Blue House in Coyoacán, which can be seen to this day.

The most frightening portrait Frida ever painted was of Irene and it is a work of terror. The drawing is called *Portrait of Irene Bohus* and is graphite on paper, executed in 1947.

The pencil drawing is an act of vicious revenge, as Irene had an affair with Diego Rivera.

This portrait shows Irene urinating into a chamber pot, which is painted with the words '*YO TI MIRO*' (I SEE YOU). In the naked portrait of Irene, she looks like a Vodou doll with phallic extensions for arms and her image is covered with tongues and long thorn-like hairs. Irene's vagina is exposed and crowned by the face of a devil.

When I asked Irene about Frida, she said, 'Frida is a mirror. She is a pool of water. Every woman sees herself in Frida.'

The minute I arrived at ten in the morning, as a ritual, Irene would serve me a glass of whisky or sherry. She never asked if I wanted to drink or not and I never refused and drank it all down. Then, with our glasses in hand, she'd guide me to her studio, where I stood by a window while she did sketches of my face, sometimes straight-on but mostly in profile. She kissed me, but I pulled away.

Irene told me she was so powerful, so electric, that she had once tamed an angry panther at the zoo in Budapest when she was a child. 'I just looked deep into the animal's eyes. It could not take my eyes.' Irene said, 'In this life, I am on the side of living things. If a little fly or bug comes inside the house, I help it escape.'

A Murder and Everything
Is in Fours

It was a small knife.

It was a very small knife with a short blade. A blade only four inches long.

To kill someone with a knife like that you have to be very close to the victim. You have to be embracing or kissing or making love.

The heart was stabbed four times.

Toward the end of my first year at boarding school, my guardian was murdered.

When I left Mexico, I'd been appointed a guardian while I was in the USA, as I was underage. The guardian was a man whose family we knew in Mexico, and who lived near the boarding school.

One weekend a month, he'd invite me to stay at his house and we'd go to a movie or he'd take me shopping. It was always a

168

treat to get out of the dorm. One Saturday, a little before midnight, he knocked on my bedroom door and said he was going out to buy some cigarettes and would be back soon. Shortly thereafter I fell asleep and didn't realise he'd never returned. I was awakened at five in the morning by the doorbell ringing over and over again. It was still dark. I went downstairs in my pajamas and opened the door. The detectives, dressed in beige trench coats, just like the cliché, carefully brushed off their shoes on the welcome mat and came into the house, pushing me to the side as they entered.

I was considered a suspect, as only a person very close to him could have committed the crime.

I was interrogated for four hours.

Detective: Where were you?
Me: In bed asleep.
Detective: Where were you?
Me: In bed asleep.
Detective: Where were you?
Me: In bed asleep.
Detective: Let me look at your hands.

I held out my hands and he looked them over, turning them around to see both sides, and looking between my fingers.

I knew he was examining them for scratch marks, knife cuts or blood.

In four, four-leaf-clover days, they caught the killer.

The day after the murder, I went back to school and classes, as 'come rain or come shine' were words to live by.

There Was No Elsewhere

Even if I had to run away to do so, I was going to go to New York City and study dance.

In our senior year everyone who was graduating from Cranbrook was filling out college applications. I applied only to the NYU dance department.

As part of the process, I had to go to an audition, which, for dancers in the Midwest of the USA, was in Chicago in the ballroom of a large hotel. I took an airplane by myself from Detroit to Chicago and stayed in the hotel where the auditions were being held.

At least two hundred dancers were being auditioned for a place at NYU that year. We'd all been told that only ten dancers would be taken. Stuart Hodes, one of Martha Graham's lead dancers and a teacher at NYU, who had also been a World War II bomber pilot, was in charge of the audition and the decision. He was supposed to sit behind a desk and watch but he kept getting up and dancing as if he were one of the dancers who were auditioning. He couldn't stop himself. He said, 'Never fight against the need to dance.'

To begin the process, the dancers were asked to do warm-up barre exercises together. Then we moved into the centre of the floor to show off our skill with standard steps. We had to do *cabrioles, jetés, pas de chat, glissés* and *glissades*. This part of the audition ended with a *révérence*.

After a short break, each dancer was called on individually to do a short dance that we'd prepared beforehand. I performed the work I'd choreographed with Waldeen, which was a dance created around the myth of the Mayan moon goddess Ixchel. My movements were round circles combined with frenzied, staccato movements, as Ixchel was both the goddess of child-birth and storms. I brought my music on a small tape recorder. It consisted of the sound of sea conches being blown like trumpets and soft, rhythmic drumming. I was one of the few who were accepted into the programme.

My parents were against my going to New York City. They wrote me many letters from Mexico and called me with urgency, trying to convince me not to go. They argued that the city was much too violent. New York had been documenting record-breaking muggings, robberies and killings. My parents urged me to go elsewhere. But, if you wanted to be a dancer or an artist, there was no elsewhere.

New York City

'I stabbed her but I never meant to kill her'

Sid Vicious, from the punk band the Sex Pistols, killed Nancy Spungen at the Chelsea Hotel with a Jaguar K-11 hunting knife. The killing was all over the front pages of the newspapers.

The radio DJs stopped playing the Bee Gees, ABBA and songs from the musical *Grease,* and played Sid Vicious's version of Frank Sinatra's 'My Way' non-stop for two days, filling up the taxis and clubs with his grizzled voice.

When he was arrested, Sid Vicious allegedly said, 'I stabbed her but I never meant to kill her.'

One month before this crime, I stayed at the Chelsea Hotel for a few days before moving into NYU housing at Brittany Hall at 10th Street and Broadway. I needed this time to buy blankets, sheets and towels for my room as well as new dance shoes before the dorm opened for the students.

The Chelsea was famous for residents such as Jackson Pollock, William Burroughs, Dylan Thomas and Bob Dylan but, when

I stayed there, I learned that the ghost of Mary, a survivor from the *Titanic*, haunted the halls after her suicide in the hotel.

The Chelsea's hallways were covered with white marble floors and there were paintings on all the walls. There was one painting of an enormous horse head. I stayed in a small room with green walls and a large armchair covered in worn green velvet. The walk-in closet, which had no window, was larger than the room.

For three days there was a lone shoe in the elevator going up and down that no one ever picked up. There were young and old sex workers who only came downstairs at night and who rented some of the rooms. Their night-time perfumes mixed in the elevator and lobby as they left to work in the city. Two old men who'd lived there for years went in and out of the elevator at all times, as if this were an activity in itself. In the lobby there was a young couple, dressed only in pink, with even pink shoes and socks, who were there when I arrived and when I left. They were surrounded by pink suitcases and smoked cigarettes non-stop, as if the hotel lobby were a train station.

To one side of the front desk, there were two phone booths with eight or nine papier-mâché figures flying above them and dangling from strings tied to a long bamboo pole. People were constantly doing drugs, dealing drugs or making out inside these phone booths.

My very first night in NYC, with five dollars in quarters, I called my father in Mexico City from one of the Chelsea Hotel phone booths. As I spoke, I read the graffiti scrawled on the metal phone with a black marker: *Don't talk or kiss for more than five minutes. Show consideration.*

She Was the Kind of Woman
Who Was Always Fainting

On the day Sid Vicious killed Nancy Spungen, I met Lili Dones at an NYU party. She looked like a 1930s movie star. Lili had golden hair, golden skin and golden eyes, and was a replica of the French actress Dominique Sanda. Lili had a lazy eye in both eyes, which meant that every few seconds her eyes were floating away. She was the kind of woman who was always fainting.

Everyone in New York City was talking about the murder and all the details that led up to the crime. Lili and I looked at each other and said, almost in unison, 'I stabbed her but I never meant to kill her.' In that instant we knew we were friends for life and for ever after knew exactly what to say whenever we made a mistake.

My first job was working the all-night shift at the Brittany Hall at NYU where I lived. Later, over the years, I worked in a blue jeans factory on Orchard Street cutting defective belt loops off blue jeans. I was the only worker there who was not Chinese. I also worked as a waitress, shop clerk, cleaning lady, bartender and babysitter.

It was when I was working at my first job in NYC at the Brittany that I got to know Lili. As she also lived in this dorm and was an insomniac, Lili would sit with me for hours until dawn.

Lili's family was from Cuba and had left their *fincas* and sugar-cane fields behind during the Cuban Revolution. Lili spoke Spanish and practised Cuban Santeria. She had an altar with seashells on a light-blue plate in her room. She said, 'My grand-mother said to have seashells in a house was bad luck, but I don't believe in this.' Lili could quote poems or verses by José Martí by heart. Her favorite quote was, 'Charm is the product of the unexpected.'

Lili's conversation was full of literary and historical allusions and wit. She once described one of her boyfriends to me, who she had thought perfect: 'And then,' she said, 'just like Lord Byron, suddenly, so suddenly, there was the club foot!'

A Dancer in New York

Every day I'd take at least four dance classes. I auditioned for the Bertram Ross Dance Company. Bertram Ross had been Martha Graham's dance partner for more than two decades and she created many roles around him.

For my dance I performed a piece I'd worked on with Waldeen over the summer holiday. It was the dance of the goddess Coyolxāuhqui, which means 'adorned with bells' in Nahuatl. The extraordinary monolith had only just been found that year in downtown Mexico City. My dance began slowly and then became violent with an enactment of the dismemberment of her limbs, as had happened to the goddess, my legs, feet, shoulders, wrists and head moving with rhythmic, staccato interludes.

After the audition, Ross called forward three dancers who had made the final cut. He lined us up at the front of the large dance room.

To one he said dramatically, 'You're like a forest fire.'

To the next dancer in the line he said, 'You? Well, you're a dumpster fire.'

To me he said, 'You're a fire in the Bronx.' In the decade of the 1970s, 80 per cent of the housing in the Bronx had burned down.

Dreaming and Nightmaring

On Thursdays, after ballet class, a small group of us would go to watch the breakdancing on Astor Place. This became a ritual during my first year studying dance in New York. Uptown they'd been having block parties for several years but by 1978 the hip-hop scene had moved downtown. A party could start up anywhere, even in a subway car or on a street corner.

Our pink tights and black leotard were still under our jeans and sweaters as we moved, poised, with our hair slicked back into a tight bun and our dance bags over our shoulders, away from the dance studios to watch the breakers. Our bodies were filled with ballet-class music. We were swans, we were nutcrackers. Standing as if we were at the barre in first position, we watched breaker crews move in shapes, flips and spins. They turned into robots, became Marcel Marceau and mimed moments from *The Three Stooges*, circus moves and walking on a tightrope. There was one move called 'dreaming' that consisted of long head spins followed by 'nightmaring', which was flips.

The breakers were bruised from many falls and they called this being 'black and blued'. These dancers had scrapes on their cheeks and hands from the rough, cold concrete sidewalks. Before the skaters took over the streets with their acrobatics, the breakers had already used ramps in their acts and some jumped off roofs and over guard rails.

Breakers got their name because of the break between songs. The DJs at parties or clubs, or those who controlled the boom boxes, began to make the breaks longer and longer to challenge the dancers. Hip-hop became the combination of deejaying, graffiti, rap and breaking. Crews were formed to compete against other crews. Once, I saw a crew dance a mugging.

This kind of dancing was intensely competitive and attitude was important, along with a sense of honour at all times. This made breaking seem like a descendant of gentlemen's fencing assaults. I once even heard a breaker cry out fencing terms as he danced. He said, '*Prêt, redoublement, remise, reposte.*'

'Revolting Music'

Minutes from the board meeting on 'Revolting Music' state:

What does REVOLTING MUSIC sound like? Well, it
isn't the vapid Barbra Streisand screeching songs
like 'People'; it isn't the wretched Sinatra's 'My
Way.'

REVOLTING MUSIC is Aretha's Respect, The Isley
Bros.' Fight the Power, and Poly Styrene's Oh
Bondage Up Yours!

REVOLTING MUSIC isn't Barry Sadler's 'Ballad of
the Green Berets.'. It isn't Billy Joel's 'I Love You
Just the Way You Are' and it definitely isn't
Reagan's 'Thumbs Up, America!'

REVOLTING MUSIC is James Brown's I Don't Want
Nobody to Give Me Nothin' (Open Up the Door and
I'll Get It Myself!). It's Vicious Rap by Sweet T.
and I'm Not Down by the Clash.

The 'Revolting Music' party began at eleven p.m. That night we danced at the Machinists' Union Hall and the only light came from a screen that projected Sergei Eisenstein's films non-stop. We danced under films that showed battleships, the Potemkin stairway in Odesa and Mexican landscapes.

Lili, along with Jenny Holzer, Julie Ault, Tim Rollins and others, became a founding member of Group Material (GM), which was based in a storefront at 244 East 13th Street. Group Materials consisted of several conceptual artists who rented the space in order to show their work. The group's statement on their vision was 'We want our work and the work of others to take a role in a broader cultural activism' and, based on this philosophy, they included the community in their shows, invitations to which were in both English and Spanish. One of their first shows was 'The People's Choice', also known as 'Arroz con Mango', which consisted of asking everyone in the neighbourhood to bring a piece of art from their own homes. One piece was a cognac glass with a small doll of a man inside who was smoking a cigarette.

The GM show 'Revolting Music' was a one-night dance party. The invitation, which was a xeroxed flyer, stated: 'Revolting Music is an exhibition of Music in the form of a wild Dance Party – FOR ONE NIGHT ONLY, GROUP MATERIAL will D.J. the revolutionary hits of the past three decades.'

Apart from Group Materials, Lili worked as a graphic designer. A few times a month we'd go to Pearl Paint to get special paper and pens she needed for her work. We liked to stop at a small paper shop on Canal Street where the owner, a kind Chinese woman who wore two very long jade hair sticks to keep her tight bun in place and who knew very little English, would allow us to xerox our bodies.

Lili and I took xeroxes of our hands and profiles by pressing our faces down on the glass and then covering our heads with a sweater, as the plastic lid did not fit. Lili used the Xerox machine to make collages.

Lili could never learn to drive or do anything that involved coordination or doing two things at the same time. She couldn't smoke a cigarette and talk. She couldn't walk and talk. I watched her try and button a blouse once and it took her so long I had to button her up as if she were my child.

Within two months of my arrival in New York City, I'd been hired as a waitress in Max's Kansas City. In New York it was almost impossible to be a waitress without prior experience or something that made you stand out. At Max's Kansas City I pretended to be French and got the job. Lili said that Tommy Dean Mills, the owner, only hired waitresses that might become someone's girlfriend.

Tommy sat at the same table every night, which was right next to the bathroom. This way he could watch the procession into the bathroom where everyone was doing coke or something. The best night was Thursday and sometimes bands like the Ramones and Blondie played at Max's. Although the New York Dolls had broken up, David Johansen was there all the time. On many nights I served Colette martinis before we became friends.

Lili would pick me up after a shift and we'd go to CBGB's or

Studio 54. There was a snobbery in New York City about weekends. We never went out to clubs on Fridays and Saturdays because this was when people from the boroughs or tourists came into New York.

Sometime that autumn we saw Elvis Costello play at CBGB's. He sang 'No Action'.

It was our anthem.

Downtown Etiquette

Among the runaways, there was a runaway etiquette: you always shared drugs, cigarettes and lipstick.

If someone was sick, you took him or her matzo ball chicken soup from the 2nd Ave Deli.

Etiquette for Studio 54
It's acceptable for you to go into Studio 54 and enjoy yourself even if your friends don't get picked at the door.

No matter what people may say on the dance floor, some words have no meaning.

Etiquette if Bill Cunningham ever gets off his bicycle and stops you on the street to ask to take your picture
Act nonchalant.

Etiquette with celebrities
Never, ever, stare at a celebrity, even if it is Kathleen Turner ordering NY strip steaks at Jefferson Market, Herman Munster

banking at Citibank on LaGuardia Place or John Kennedy Jr talking in a phone booth near Judson Hall.

Etiquette for parting favours

It's acceptable to hand parting dinner guests your garbage bag so they can drop it off outside.

Etiquette at restaurants

You can smoke at a restaurant but never if someone at your table is actually eating. Best restaurants to smoke and drink and not eat are Evelyn's Kitchen, Odeon, Raoul's and Mr. Chow.

Etiquette for violence:

You always lend your crowbar, hammer and cut-off broomstick if someone has to walk home late at night.

A kind of homemade pepper spray was shared around, a combination of pepper mixed with hot chilli powder. We carried it in plastic bags that you could get from a club doorman for a dollar.

One young woman who used to walk around Alphabet City with an electrical cattle prod held out in front of her said she was happy to take orders if anyone wanted one. She grew up on a farm with cows in the Midwest.

Two Shadowmen

Being a dancer was being a runaway. I could leave my home and go to the white room covered with mirrors and dance for the metamorphosis into swan, dance to be a fairy, dance to become deer and moon.

After being in New York for three months, I woke up from a dream and knew I had to leave dance. Just like that. But for ever after I could not sit through a dance concert without my body aching for it and feeling an absence of myself. And for ever after I would be fascinated by stories and myths about people who acted on a message in dreams. The dream showed me that dancing was child's play. In the dream I walked through a wood of saplings. The tall trees were only shadows of trees.

The afternoon following the dream I walked over to 2nd Street and Houston. There, along one side of the building, were two crime scenes painted to look like they were people who had fallen from the roof in mid suicide. Beside these figures someone had spray-painted the word 'DSIRE'.

During 1978, throughout the Lower East Side, Richard Hambleton had painted crimes scenes before he became better known for his Shadowmen on walls or inside subway stations.

On sidewalks, or on the black asphalt of the city streets, Richard drew the outline of corpses with white paint to look like police chalk drawn around a victim. At first, I would just stand and look in silence and reverence at these outlines on the ground and wonder who had died there, until I understood that they were street art.

Anytime Lili and I came across one of these crime drawings, we would get inside them as a ritual participation. We took turns lying down on the cold cement, holding the death pose. We'd fit like a puzzle piece with one arm stretched out, one leg bent backward, our faces in profile facing north.

After the dream of leaving dance, I lay inside the crime drawing.

I had fallen from a bullet.

I had fallen from a midnight knifing.

I had fallen from an airplane.

'Fuck Art Let's Dance'

Colette was a mermaid out of the water. Her soft voice, singing tenderly, was out of breath, full of breeze, in slow-motion:

> The evening breeze caressed the trees tenderly
> The trembling trees embraced the breeze tenderly

Colette's fashion was what she called Victorian Punk, which was a punk aesthetic that had vintage elegance and was extremely feminine.

When I first got to New York, I would walk over to the Fiorucci store, as Colette did installations in the shop's window. These live performances would last for days. Once, I watched Colette sleep, in one of her public sleeping performances, covered in lace and velvet blankets outside on the stairs of a building.

The first time I saw Colette perform was at Danceteria. That night she performed the living tableaux 'Fuck Art Let's Dance', which was an installation of Colette half-naked. She sang and moved slowly on the small stage along with Rudolf Pieper.

Colette was one of the first artists on the New York scene who created videos. With Jeff Koons as the protagonist, she filmed *Justine and the Boys*. This film has three other titles: *Notes on Baroque Living, Too Much Is Not Enough* and, recently added by her, *A Historical Hysterical Tape, Documenting A 'Real Life' Part of Art History – Before Reality Shows Existed*.

The video opens with Colette arriving at her apartment off the street and getting straight into a water-filled bathtub while still wearing a corset, her shoes and two hats. The tub is enveloped in gauze and looks like a small sea. In the foreground there is a vase of flowers and a large shell. In the tub she has a conversation with Jeff Koons while he flips casually through a magazine, perched on the edge of the tub fully dressed. Colette gets ready for 'the boys' who are coming to visit. While applying blue nail polish to her fingernails, the telephone rings.

Jeff answers, 'We're busy', and hangs up.

Colette asks, 'Did you ask who it was?'

Jeff replies, 'He said an ex.'

'Ex?' Colette repeats. 'That's very funny,' she says and giggles. 'I wonder who that was. Ex? Certainly not a prince.'

In 2016, Colette and I, along with other artists and writers, were invited to South Africa to create art for an auction to support the Swedish Star for Life charity to help children with AIDS in KwaZulu-Natal. This project was headed by the Swedish artist Johan Falkman, who also has strong ties to New York and Mexico.

In South Africa, Colette and I rediscover each other. We look into a mirror and see ourselves again for the first time. After the safari, on which we looked into the eyes of elephants and lions, Colette and I remember Cindy Sherman, Jeff Koons, Basquiat and Warhol. We recall the nights in New York City at Club 57, the Mudd Club, Danceteria and Pyramid.

One afternoon as we wait for an official visit from the Zulu king and his entourage, which includes his many wives, we watch Colette's film *Justine and the Boys* on my phone in a jeep parked under a fever tree. She says, 'I don't think I've ever been able to make my face look angry.'

When Colette speaks, I know she's 'The Mermaid in the Attic', 'Liberty Leading the People', 'Mata Hari and the Stolen Potatoes' and 'Lumiere'. These are all the characters she has created as personas, which she embodies in her live installations.

From this trip to South Africa, there is a photograph of Colette reading my book *Widow Basquiat* whilst leaning on an enormous stuffed lioness. It was taken inside a small grass-thatched hut in which she created the installation called 'Les Trésors de L'Afrique /Lumiere in Zululand'.

In the hut, sitting on the floor, next to the lioness, we remember living with AIDS in NYC in the early 1980s. It's a strange circle, a strange game of dot-to-dot from New York City to KwaZulu-Natal.

Colette says, 'I can't believe we didn't get it.'

Then she names the names like a chant:

Cookie Mueller

Klaus Nomi

Keith Haring

Dondi

Haoui Montaug

Roswell, who once said his favorite colour was plaid.
Tina Chow
And Gina, Steve, Bree, Romana, Kevin, Brooke, Alan and and and and

'I know,' I answer. 'We thought sex was freedom and then it was death.'

Colette says, 'Sleep, death and love is what matters.'

Only a few steps away we can hear the purr of lions and the strangled yips of the hyenas who follow the lions.

When I try and remember when things happened, Colette answers, 'I have no idea. I only know my life by boyfriends. They are my landmarks.'

I say, 'I always think everything happened to me when I was eleven years old.'

One afternoon I ask a driver named Ziggy to take me to a far-off village to visit a sangoma. As we drive in a jeep toward the Lebombo Mountains, Ziggy tries to explain what a sangoma is. He says, 'She is a not a fortune-teller, she is more like a diviner who tells you about your whole life. The diviner is a spiritual person. She sees something in you.'

The sangoma waits for me in a round, empty hut. She is an old and tall woman with grey hair and small, very kind, light-brown eyes. She's barefoot and tells me to take off my shoes and sit beside her on a straw mat on the floor. The sangoma gives me a bottle filled with water and I hold it in silence for ten minutes before she takes it from my hands and chants in Zulu. After praying, the sangoma's eyes fill with tears and then she begins to cry in earnest, with tears rolling down her cheeks. She has to wipe her nose with her sleeve. Then I cry with her and we weep together in the silence of the hut. After a while she says that my ancestral sadness can only be cured by having a sorrow party for my children and friends.

No premonition came to me that I would find my childhood friend in KwaZulu-Natal. There was never a dream-come-true dream or tightly-squeezed-fist wish, but he was there too, painting an enormous rhinoceros and studies of small pineapples for the Star for Life charity. It was Pedro Diego Alvarado Rivera, my childhood friend. He brought Ruth María to South Africa in his eyes, in his grandfather's face and in his kind, open heart. Ruth María had already been dead for nine years. The last time I saw her was at a party in Mexico City in 2006. When she saw me from across the garden, she sat right up and moved toward me in her awkward, long strides. In her embrace, I could still feel her strong desire to carry me, kiss me and feel again that I was a part of her body. We sat together and drank tequila and she told me she was dying. I will always belong to her.

The skies of Mexico opened over South Africa.

Querencia

It was like living in Hansel and Gretel's gingerbread house. My apartment on 13 St Mark's Place between Second and Third Avenue, above the St Mark's bookstore, was made for a fairy tale. The stairs going up to it, on the fourth floor, were covered in murals that were landscapes of woodlands and small flowers. The red doors to the apartments were carved with woodcuts in shapes of hearts, half-moons and four-leaf clovers, like cookie cutters.

For a year, every Sunday, I hosted an evening poetry workshop at my St Mark's apartment.

The teacher who gave the workshop was a poet and my professor at the NYU English department. He made us memorise a poem every week because he believed that memorising poems was important and even a lost art. I memorised poems by Yeats, Whitman and Neruda. I also memorised Gabriela Mistral's poem 'The Dancer', as it spoke to many of my feelings about giving up my life as a dancer in those days:

The dancer is now dancing
the dance of losing everything she had.

196

The professor asked us to write down what poetry meant to each of us. I wrote: 'poetry is close to my dreams and where my desires come true'.

One evening, after all the poetry workshop students had left, the professor stayed on. He was handsome, with deep-set blue eyes. We drank beer and he told me about a woman, a stranger, he met at a shop in Hiroshima. He said they looked at each other and had instantly fallen in love. Thereafter he longed for her, even though they'd only seen each other for a few moments.

He asked if I'd ever felt this way. As he spoke, I never wondered why he was telling me this. I touched his cheek. I kissed him. We were together for the next three years.

Although I did not answer his question about love at first sight, I had felt this kind of instant love-belonging once. It happened to me with an actor who was in Peter Brook's company, which had come to Mexico to perform *Ubu Roi* in the summer of 1978. I had graduated from boarding school and was waiting to go to New York in September. This was the summer that Jacques Lecoq and Donato Sartori also came to Mexico. Barbara and I took their mask-making and mime workshops. Together Sartori and Lecoq created a happening in the Plaza Santa Catarina in Coyoacán. This consisted of one of Sartori's *Mascheramento Urbano* (Urban Masks). The square was covered in thin muslin, which turned the whole space into a massive spider web. Barbara and I, along with others, performed a work created by Jacques Lecoq there. The Mexican actress Jesusa Rodríguez was the star.

On one night during the Peter Brook company's run, Waldeen's dancers were invited to a cocktail party for the visiting actors at a house in Desierto de los Leones, in the south of Mexico City. The house had a very large and over-grown garden with brambles of ancient rose bushes everywhere. I went out to the garden and, walking among the vines and wild weeds, I came across Bruce Myers. He stood by himself with his hands behind his back and his head tilted backward, looking up at the sky where not a single star could be seen in the dense city smog. This was twelve years before he would play the roles of Ganesha and Krishna in Brook's movie *The Mahabharata*.

I watched as Bruce moved slowly toward the garden path and toward me. There was something I wanted to say to him, but the words wouldn't let me. I was eighteen and he was thirty-five. When we looked at each other, our hearts were two clash cymbals that struck together. Just like that.

Maybe this kind of love is like a *querencia*. In a bullfight, the *querencia* is the bull's instinctive and immediate attachment to a particular area of the bullring the minute he is let loose, and the only place the animal feels safe – a mix of tenderness and desire for love. The matador needs to find the place quickly and make it inhospitable by claiming that terrain for himself. This makes the bull lose his power.

Later I saw Bruce in New York, and then again in Paris, and the *querencia* was always there.

In the drafts of poems written in those days, I wrote three lines for Bruce, which would later be a part of a poem in my first book of poems:

All within me waits for him
As I suck on a pomegranate
The only fruit that has teeth.

Valentine's Day Chocolates

By the fall of 1979, I had left NYU's dance department and was enrolled at NYU's Gallatin Division, where I was studying literature and anthropology and going to poetry workshops at the English department.

That year my NYU professor, and chair of the anthropology department, Professor John Buettner-Janusch, was caught making LSD with students at an NYU laboratory. Professor Buettner-Janusch was convicted of making both LSD and methaqualone and jailed.

On 14 February 1987, he sent Valentine chocolates laced with poison to the judge who had convicted him and was jailed again.

Poetry Nights

One night after I'd waitressed the graveyard shift, a man was stabbed to death. His body lay on the pavement in front of my building. He was dressed in a gold and blue sequinned evening gown. I had to step over him to get inside.

Those of us who lived on the Lower East Side, Alphabet City and below Houston Street would furnish our small apartments with chairs, sofas and tables that had been set out on the sidewalk for the garbage trucks to take away. One armchair I took from the corner of Avenue A and 7th Street. Lili and two other friends helped carry it to my apartment. When I lifted up the pillow, I found dozens of lost, half-used crayons there like relics.

Crime was so random and constant that in February 1979 Curtis Silwa founded the Guardian Angels. Their groups patrolled the streets and subway stations and cars. They wore red bomber jackets and red berets so they could be easily identified. All the girls thought they were very sexy.

The drag bar on the corner filled the night with the sounds of Donna Summer singing 'Bad Girls', which opens and ends with the rhythmic sound of a police whistle. Outside the place there were constant sidewalk fights and shouting. Once, at about three in the morning, I heard someone outside my window screaming for twenty minutes, 'That was my tiara, you mother-fucker!'

The block was dark at night because all the streetlights had been shot out.

I gave my first poetry reading at Keith Haring's Wednesday Poetry Nights at Club 57 on St Mark's Place. On Keith's flyers these readings were advertised as 'A Non-Writers Poetry Reading'. The flyers were copied at Todd's Copy Shop on Mott Street, where many of us spent our time, as xeroxing everything was exciting and revolutionary. Keith glued his flyers on lamp-posts and walls. The xeroxing of announcements, rent opportunities and love letters became a part of the graffiti street landscape.

The only thing that was not glued over, and was respected by all, was the face of Etan Patz. Years after his disappearance in May 1979, his six-year-old face still appeared on flyers stuck to lampposts and phone booths.

Sometimes Keith's flyers, which he also made for his art shows, would feature a no-show just to draw people in. The very first Poetry Night flyer I was featured on also announced readings by Keith Haring and Arthur Rimbaud. Rimbaud did not show up.

Once, on my way to one of Keith's readings, I fell down in the street and cut open my hand. When I arrived at Club 57, Keith took me into the bathroom and lathered up his hands and washed both of mine, holding them under the faucet. I had not had my hands washed by someone since childhood. It made me remember the feeling of someone putting on my socks and tying up my shoes. It made me feel sleepy, little-girl sleepy. Keith had tenderness in him, the tenderness that one finds in jails and hospitals.

Across the street from my apartment was a secondhand store known as Andy's Chee-Pees, where I bought vintage clothes. For my first poetry reading, I went to Andy's and bought a black velvet dress that had faded yellow plastic seed pearls sewn into the collar. The dress had an old tag sewn into the back, the kind that is sewn into children's sweaters, with the name 'Gloria Swanson'. It cost me ten dollars. I also wore ankle-high, black stiletto-heeled boots, black gloves and black fishnet stockings with large holes in both knees.

On this night, the first person to read was a young man who said it was his twenty-first birthday. He read a poem about a children's party, which ended with the line, 'I only wanted to pop the balloons. Pop. Pop. Pop.'

Keith, who was very sweet and shy, read his own Neo-Dada poems over and over again in different combinations behind a fake television set held up to his face as if he were in the TV. In his soft, slightly nasal voice he said:
    'I am the other one.'

I read a poem called 'What Lives Do I Live in Other People's Dreams?'

Box for One Sock Found

Our main outfit was red lipstick.

On Thursday nights Lili, who by then had also moved out of the NYU dorm to an apartment on 7th Street, and I would go to Pyramid, which was mostly a gay and transvestite club. Lili dressed like a 1940s movie star, with a tight bodice, wide skirt with a crinoline and slingback sandals. The advantage we had over many was that we could gossip about everyone in Spanish.

Next door to Pyramid was Kim's Cleaners, where we did our laundry. In our high heels and holding on to our cocktails, we'd rush back and forth between the club and the laundromat as our clothes went through the cycles.

Kim's Cleaners had a box filled with socks and, on one side, someone had written with a marker 'Box for one sock found'. The large warm room smelled of chlorine and Tide and rotten oranges. Rotten oranges were a part of the constant New York City downtown smell. Static-cling-away cloths lay about the floor and inside dryers. There was a day-old *New York Post* lying on a counter or a fashion magazine we could read. Kim's

Cleaners closed at midnight. There were signs on the wall that said 'No chairs' and 'Don't get comfortable'.

Once Pyramid became more successful, the laundromat also became more successful and everyone was running back and forth between sets. Kim's Cleaners became a place to drink cocktails and talk and cry over a breakup.

Diana Ross, a transvestite who did her laundry there during breaks in the show at Pyramid, once said, 'If nothing else in this life, our clothes at least are clean.' She placed her dresses covered in sequins in the washer and dryer.

In those days broken-off red and gold sequins were always stuck to my clothes.

TV Party

On Tuesday nights, NYC's Lower East Side came to a stop as everyone was in front of a television set watching *TV Party*, a live cocktail party on cable television. It was on from twelve-thirty to one-thirty a.m. and Glenn O'Brien was both the creator and host. He modelled his act on the Johnny Carson and Ed Sullivan talk shows, with a live audience and a band called the TV Party orchestra, which mostly featured Lenny Ferrari. The show was so successful Blondie references it in her 1981 song 'Rapture'.

Glenn had a long and complicated manifesto on what *TV Party* was all about. A TV Party, he explained, was both a cocktail party and a political party, and that a party happened automatically if *TV Party* was turned on.

His *TV Party* manifesto made clear that what was happening that night on television was happening in your own life. The party could even be shared by calling up someone on the telephone and watching it together while talking or dancing.

The manifesto also stated that a *TV Party* was the 'highest expression of social activity' and the most exquisite form of co-operative fun.

Tetracycline

He was more beautiful than Marlene Dietrich or Björn Johan Andrésen, who played Tadzio in Visconti's *Death in Venice*.

Hal Ludacer was the most beautiful creature in New York. I met Hal the very first month of my first year in the city. I was working at the front desk at Brittany Hall late one night and he arrived like a knight, carrying in his arms the limp body of a young woman who'd passed out from drugs and alcohol. He took the girl up to his room and nursed her. I adored him immediately.

Hal and I became inseparable. He was tall and wore black, narrow jeans with a tucked-in white shirt. Sometimes he would wear make-up and black eyeliner. For the almost non-existent acne he imagined on his face, he lived on tetracycline and popped the antibiotic pills all day long as if they were mints.

My get-up was a very feminine punk princess aesthetic. I had black dresses and one very large black taffeta skirt, which the seamstress had made for me in Mexico and rustled when I walked. Part of this look included three strands of plastic pearls I roped around my neck and wrists. My lips were painted with cherry-red or black-red lipstick.

A few nights a week, we'd go to Studio 54 and then to the Mudd Club. We'd have a long night-time nap and then get up and get ready. We did this so we'd be the last to arrive everywhere. The doormen at the clubs always let us in.

Hal and I had our own unique way of dancing together. While everyone else was moving frenetically around the dance floor to the B-52's or the Ramones playing live, he and I would stand almost completely still, moving very slightly. Hal's left shoulder would go up and down with his toes turned inward. My hips would only slightly sway in a circular motion. Our dance was a dance of statues.

Hal liked to buy me presents. He gave me a pair of vintage pink gloves that went up the length of my arms. He bought me a rhinestone necklace and a rhinestone bracelet shaped like a chain of leaves. Hal gave me a copy of Nico's 1967 album *Chelsea Girl*, which we listened to all the time.

Even though we went out a lot, Hal and I were really loners, which was why were such good friends: we were alone together in the crowd, keeping watch over each other's solitude. After the night – now morning – was over, we'd go back to my apartment and sleep nestled together in my bed like children taking a nap after Kool-Aid and cookies.

I first met Andy Warhol one night with Hal, who already knew him, at Studio 54. He greeted Hal and just like that slid his hand down the front of Hal's trousers and felt him up, which was something he did whenever he wanted. I felt very protective of Hal because he was pestered by other old creeps all the time and, since he was only seventeen, a year younger than me, was vulnerable to this strange ownership older men seemed to feel they had over his body. Andy was the worst. He really harassed Hal, as if his fame and fortune gave him rights. We kept away from Andy as much as possible.

Warhol had phrases he'd roll out as bits of wisdom, such as something to the effect that life only has atmosphere when it's a memory. Hal explained to me once that some of Andy's mystery, or even perceived intelligence, had a lot to do with the fact that he never answered a question. Andy stayed absolutely quiet or answered with one of his set retorts.

Between 1983 and 1984, Jean-Michel Basquiat drew forty-five amusing, sorrowful and unforgiving portraits of artists on plates. For the one of Andy, Jean-Michel wrote 'BOY GENIUS' under the portrait, which exposes Andy's sardonic cruelty. In the introductory text in a book of Jean-Michel's portrait plates, Francesco Clemente writes with his sharp insight and wit that the portraits express '. . . the sublime silence of Cimabue, Matisse's achievements of late collages, Picasso's relentless eye, Keith Haring's graphic sex machine, Andrew Wyeth's all-American pastoral utopia, Larry Rivers' Painterly machism, Francesco Clemente's vain fear of death, Marisol's ecstatic gaze, Louise Nevelson's austerity, Jasper Johns' diamond-cut spirit, fame-hungry Julian Schnabel.'

The last party held at Studio 54 was called the 'The End of Modern-day Gomorrah'. The party was held on 2 February

1980, the night before Steve Rubell and Ian Schrager went to jail for tax fraud. Hal and I went to the party, where the male waiters dressed only in Calvin Klein underwear and handed out coke for free in black plastic film containers. The waiters would say, 'Here, powder your nose.' The bar was open and Gloria Gaynor's 'I Will Survive' was played over and over again. Steve Rubell sang 'My Way'.

Hal and I were there because that night it was the only place to be on Earth.

Hal and I went to the first screening in New York of John Waters' movie *Polyester*, in which Divine had the main part. At the premiere at the Waverly, in the West Village, we were given scratch-n-sniff cards so that we could smell what was happening in the movie, as Divine's character, Francine Fishpaw, was obsessed with household odours. A number would flash on the screen and the audience would know what to smell on the card.

This is the list:
Roses
Flatulence (Natural ass)
Model airplane glue
Pizza
Gasoline
Skunk
Natural gas
New car smell
Dirty shoes
Air freshener

211

Divine, although almost always acting a female persona and who loved to be in drag, identified as male. Hilarious and sweet and cruel, he was always on the frontier between laughter and tears. He gave me his vintage black mink fur coat one night, which I wore all through the winter of 1981. I lost it when it fell from my hands as I was getting into a taxi after dancing most of the night to Sylvester's 'You Make Me Feel (Mighty Real)'. I was so drunk and high, I couldn't coordinate to reach down and pick up the coat and so I left it there on the cold cement sidewalk where, in my mind, it still lies for ever after, one door down from Paradise Garage on King Street.

People Who Are Not
in This Book

The Parties of the Famous Deaths were organised by Lili at her apartment on 7th Street. For the first party, Lili went as Marie Antoinette in a gown and white wig she bought at a wig shop on Broadway, to which she added lots of white cotton to make it more voluptuous.

The guillotine was homemade. Lili used pieces of cardboard covered with aluminum foil, which tied at the back of her neck in a bow and which she wore all night long. I went as Isadora Duncan, with a long scarf fashioned by knotting silk scarves together around my neck. At a bike shop I borrowed a bicycle tyre, as a stand-in for a car's tyre, which I carried over my arm like an enormous bracelet.

So many people came to these parties that we didn't fit in Lili's small apartment and so spilled out into the hallways. After a few hours and many drinks, even the elevator became a part of the party space, with couples taking turns going up and down the eight floors non-stop. I said it was the place where people who should not be together were together.

At another Famous Deaths party Lili went as the Mexican actress Lupe Vélez, who had been married to Johnny Weissmuller and had killed herself by taking seventy-five Seconal pills with a glass of brandy. Lili wore a long, silky, gold nightgown and carried a roll of toilet paper with her at all times, as some claimed that Lupe Vélez actually died by falling into the toilet, she was so out of it, and drowning.

To this party I went as the Mexican poet Rosario Castellanos and held a small bedside lamp in one hand, as Castellanos, when ambassador for Mexico in Israel, had been electrocuted by touching a lamp when she was still wet from her bath. The party favours I handed out to everyone were xeroxes with my favourite lines from her poem 'Self Portrait':

> But crying
> Is in me a broken mechanism
> and I don't cry in the burial chamber
> neither at the sublime occasion nor in the face of
>   catastrophe.
> I cry when I burn the rice . . .

Curare Poison

'I have enough curare here to poison all of New York City,' Dr Robert Carneiro said, pointing to four large jars of brown paste standing on the floor to one side of his desk. 'This is why I keep it close and I can't leave this room until it gets placed under lock and key.'

Curare is the dark-brown poisonous paste used on arrows and blow darts among the Indigenous people in some areas of South America. It induces paralysis.

Dr Carneiro was the curator of South American ethnology at the American Museum of Natural History in New York. For more than a year while studying at NYU, I was his intern.

Some of my professors and older students at the anthropology department told me that it was incredibly hard to get a job at the museum, where many of us wanted to work, and that one way in was to become a guide, for which there was also a long waiting list.

One morning, and only out of curiosity, I went up to the

information desk in the middle of the museum's massive entry hall. I explained to the woman who was working behind the general information desk that I wanted a job there. She looked me up and down and, when I told her I could speak Spanish, made a telephone call and then told me to go straight up to Robert Carneiro's office.

In this first meeting, we spoke about Mexico, South America and poetry and Dr Carneiro, a giant figure in the history of cultural anthropology, hired me on the spot to be his assistant on two of his projects.

Dr Carneiro was born of Cuban parents and was an exceptionally kind man with soft, luminous brown eyes and a brilliant mind and a fidelity to factual data and scientific protocols. Under his supervision, I learned the techniques for rigorous research and the value of empirical science. He and I shared a love of myth and poetry. The project he gave me was to study the eating taboos of the tribes in the Amazon in order to find out if eating taboos were protein-related or not. Most of the books I needed to consult on these topics were at Columbia University or at the New York Public Library.

Dr Carneiro was one of the people in charge of remodelling the Amazonian exhibit in the Hall of South American Peoples. I assisted him in the creation of the exhibition on the hunting implements of the Amazon. This work allowed me to explore the immense rooms, which were like warehouses, filled with shelves and immense drawers, in the floors below the public exhibition halls. In one drawer, I found arrows that were eight to ten feet long made by the Sirionó from eastern Bolivia, which are thought to be the longest arrows in the world. Dr Carneiro completed the hall in 1989.

As I studied the diet and weapons of the Amazon, I was in the land where my mother's youngest brother, Russell, lived among the Kayapo tribe by the Xingu River in the easternmost part of the Amazon rainforest. My uncle fell in love with the Amazon and lived there for decades until his death. Russell talked about the fish and birds and rainbows as if he were the first man to ever see this landscape or as if he were true kin to Pedro Álvares Cabral or Amerigo Vespucci. My uncle said there was nothing to match the dawn with the sun lighting up the red and blue feathers of the macaw. He was made a tribal chief. This honour was given to him for coaching the tribe's football team, which allowed the Kayapo to win their first game ever against a neighbouring tribe.

I never slept. I lived on coffee, coke, Coca-Cola and Camels. I worked as a waitress, studied literature and anthropology at NYU, went to Studio 54 and the Mudd Club on Thursday nights, went to Club 57 on Wednesdays. I took poetry workshops and dance classes, read about the eating taboos among the Amazon tribes and spent time in the vast halls and rooms under the museum looking over its collection of hunting implements and selecting the best examples. As I walked the streets of Manhattan, the Amazon walked with me.

In the myths and songs from the Amazon, I gathered material for my writing. I made lists, such as the names of girls from the Eastern Timbira tribe: Stargirl, Girl of the Blossom, Small Fish, Road Up A Mountain, Crocodile Girl, Beautiful Head, Painted Lower Leg.

I kept a record of myths. The Tucano believe that night was created when the sun gave the tribe a secret bag and told them not to ever open it. When they disobeyed, millions of small black ants came out of the bag and turned the sky black.

All songs come in dreams, according to the Xavante peoples. The songs are accessed by waking up boys in the hope of hearing a song they might be dreaming.

The relationship between hunter and prey was often erotic and, in some tribes, the verb to hunt could be translated as 'to make love to the animals'. Because of this, there was a need for abstinence before the hunt and the hunter had to sexually excite the game through songs or movements so that the animal would draw near and allow itself to be killed. The poems I wrote that year were influenced by all these studies:

Before he leaves to go hunting, he will not touch me,
fearing to make them jealous: the monkey, the jaguar,
    the deer.
I too am jealous of the animals
before he returns, on that night, I clean his arrows.

'Travelers', a poem I wrote at this time, appeared in the *American Poetry Review*:

We need the unknown landscape where the moon is
    hunted,
hunted like a jaguar, bear and squirrel,
and the night is arrow-poisoned black with curare.
Songs sound like rain, fish swim the air and comets,

218

mercury-tailed comets, rip open the sky. Forever
   moving,
we share the acrobat's call
for the highwire-skywalk
who, like all stars, seek the falling.

In my notebooks, I wrote: 'Reading is still a revelation. In the quiet silence of reading, I know my solitude. I remember the wonder as a child – like a magic trick – of learning to read without speaking the words aloud and hearing the silent words – the silent books – inside myself.'

In my notes I also wrote a contemplation on the work I was doing and quoted Karl Marx from *Pre-Capitalist Economic Formations*. I read Janet Siskind's book *To Hunt in the Morning* and studies by the heroic Brazilian activists Orlando and Cláudio Villas-Bôas, who in 1961 were instrumental in getting the whole of the Xingu legally protected:

> In our modest opinion, the true defense of the Indian is to respect him and to guarantee his existence according to his own values. Until we, the 'civilized' ones, create the proper conditions among ourselves for the future integration of the Indians, any attempt to integrate them is the same as introducing a plan for their destruction. We are not yet sufficiently prepared.

. . .

As a present to Dr Carneiro for his birthday, I collected a small dictionary of words for him in Nahuatl, since he was interested in learning more about the language:

Tezcatlipoca: a mirror that smokes and sighs

Chochcanenqui: to pretend to be asleep

Choquizotlahua: exhaustion from weeping

A Song

Yambatani koro kutopoti idyako yumbo apo'inyedeto pawaidye pote potoyo

Do not look into my face that way, for, if you do, I shall never be able to forget you.

Song of the Caribs in Guyana

Paris 1

In 1867, Victor Hugo wrote a letter to Mexico's president, Benito Juárez, begging for him to save the life of Emperor Maximilian. The letter discussed the ethics and the abolishment of the death penalty as a 'Law of Light'. The missive arrived too late, exactly one day after the emperor's execution on 19 June 1867.

As part of the letter, Victor Hugo wrote, 'You have just defeated monarchies with democracy. You showed them the power so show your beauty now. After lightning, show the aurora.' These arguments had already been formed in Hugo's unsuccessful attempt to stop the execution of the abolitionist John Brown in the United States.

In Mexico this story about Victor Hugo's letter was legendary. In addition, if you were a poet or an artist in Mexico, one felt the presence of France everywhere, in the figures of André Breton, Antonin Artaud and, more recently, J. M. G. Le Clézio, who were a part of Mexico, as were artists such as Henri Cartier-Bresson. We read poems by Guillaume Apollinaire, who had

222

been kept informed on Mexico because his brother had lived and died in Mexico City, and we studied his ideas on Cubism and Surrealism.

When my advisor at New York University suggested I spend a semester in Paris studying French literature, I immediately said yes. In Mexico City the stories of Diego Rivera and Octavio Paz in France, along with many others, were a key part of the famous transatlantic friendships that existed throughout the twentieth century. Mexico's president, Porfirio Díaz, was buried in Montparnasse and Paz's admiration for Stephane Mallarmé, his multiplicity of selves, and most especially his poem 'Un coup de dés', inspired a notable following among Mexico's poets. The effect of Mallarmé on Mexican poetry, working through Paz, could almost be called a movement.

The first week in Paris, my mother, who was visiting, said she'd like to take a series of photographs of me among the graves at the Père-Lachaise cemetery. We spent two whole days taking photographs. I had to change clothes inside abandoned crypts.

Years later, her work as a photographer was exhibited when she recorded, in 2001, the historic graffiti that appeared all over Mexico City on the arrival of the leader of the Zapatistas, Subcomandante Marcos and the Zapatistas. They walked in the 'March of the Color of the Earth' for more than 3,000 kilometres from Chiapas to Mexico City to state their demands for equality for Mexico's Indigenous peoples. My mother was almost run over by cars on two occasions as she captured hundreds of historic images on busy highways and streets, which, for a year, changed the urban landscape of Mexico City.

Paris 2

In Paris I had a French boyfriend who belonged to an aristocratic family. I met him at a party for a Colombian fashion
designer. A month later, my boyfriend was in Spain visiting his
sister and so he couldn't come to a party we'd been invited to
in the country. I went without him and was given a lift by a
couple who had just bought a new car. When I arrived at their
flat with a small weekend bag for the five days, I was surprised
and worried to see they had packed six suitcases and had three
pairs of dress shoes with wooden shoe trees inside. Nobody had
told me that the country house was near a casino where the
nights would be spent getting dressed up to go out gambling,
drinking and dancing.

As we travelled out into the country, the man, François, who
was driving, spent the whole journey bragging about his new
car. After a two-hour trip, we arrived at the house. François'
passion for his new car was immediately silenced by a beautiful,
forest-green Jaguar convertible with golden-brown leather seats
that was parked in the clearing in front of the entrance. We
were told the car belonged to a Baron from an old aristocratic
French family who had come to spend a few days with us.

Immediately the five sets of couples who'd been invited became enchanted with the Baron and he and his car became the centre of attention and adulation. The following day, the owner of the country house told us he was sad to say that his cousin, who was a priest, would be joining us. He told us the priest was a bore and was very apologetic and hoped this would not ruin our time at his home.

When the priest arrived everyone ignored him and some of the guests were outright rude. At one point, over breakfast, someone even told a dirty nun joke. I began to feel uneasy and sorry for the priest. In the evening, as everyone got dressed up and went to the casino to dance and drink and play the tables, I stayed back with the priest, as I had not packed evening clothes.

The priest and I dined together alone and sometimes walked outside in the gardens under the trees or stayed inside quietly reading in side-by-side armchairs. In our talks, we discussed the difference between being a missionary and an anthropologist and the difference between converting or respecting an Indigenous culture's beliefs. As the days went by, the fawning over the Baron became worse and worse and everyone wanted to go for a ride in his fabulous car. The priest and I were mostly ignored.

And then the trick happened. I was in an Alexandre Dumas novel.

On the night before we were leaving, over drinks after dinner, the owner asked everyone to be quiet as he had an announcement to make. He said a trick had been played and it had all come out even better than expected. He said that he'd decided to create a surprise, a game, a joke.

'Nothing is what it seems,' he said. 'The priest is the Baron and the person who is pretending to be the Baron is my cousin just playing the role.'

There was no laughter or fun.

The room became a house of mirrors.

And everyone was quiet and there was a feeling of terrible fury. It was as if the trick, was an evil mirror everyone had to look into and see who they were. Everyone could see their huge heads and tiny mouths, round bellies and long necks. When they smiled, the faces frowned. When they laughed, the faces cried.

The five couples left that very night and I stayed behind with the Baron and the owner of the house.

For the rest of my stay, I drove around the French countryside with the Baron. He offered me cigarettes and we both smoked quietly, as if the smoke leaving our mouths was words we were speaking. When we finished, we both threw our cigarette butts out of the Jaguar's windows. The best thing about smoking in those smoking days was that smoke always replaced conversation.

Paris 3

Scraps from the Paris Diaries:

Hal comes to visit in Paris. At night he snuggles up close to me without knowing it. Or does he? He sleeps with his head on my chest and his arms around me.

Dominique, my French boyfriend, asks me if there is a secret on which my whole life depends. We fight all the time and then he asks me to marry him. I say no and feel like an echo: no no no no.

Hal reads my diary without permission. He reads my reading notes with quotes from *Madame Bovary*, 'The denigration of those we love always severs us from them a little', and from Balzac, 'A man ought not to marry without having studied anatomy, and dissected at least one woman', and even reads my notes on Molière's ideas on tobacco. To this, Hal writes in my diary in his quick scrawl, 'Everyone you write about is a monster.'

Last night I had dinner with Robert, who is Matisse's

great-grandson and is a little older than me. He knows all about the catacombs under Paris. Yesterday morning, in the woods somewhere outside of the city, he hunted and shot the pheasant we ate, which he cooked with a delicious onion purée. We ate in a dining room surrounded by Matisses on every wall.

The white linen napkin lay across my lap like a flag of surrender. He did not know.

I am twenty. Where will I go?

Paris 4

'Ten pieces, my heart has been broken into ten pieces,' is almost the first thing my ex-boyfriend from New York says when he comes to visit me in Paris. He does not stay with me.

He'd been in a band that played at many of the NYC clubs. I'd promoted the band, or sometimes did the lights at the gigs, but for a few months in 1979 I was mostly the girlfriend at the table to the right of the stage.

He said, 'I never loved you.'

I said, 'I loved you. In any case, I might as well be a stranger now. You don't know me any more.'

But our bodies knew each other and even our shadows greeted each other with kindness.

This story is only important because I learned that the body can remember what the heart has forgotten. Knee to knee, hip to hip, arm to arm and mouth to mouth, we fit like teeth in a zipper.

Lightning Strikes Again

THE NEW YORK TIMES

RARE CANCER SEEN IN 41 HOMOSEXUALS
By Lawrence K. Altman
July 3, 1981

Doctors in New York and California have diagnosed among homosexual men 41 cases of a rare and often rapidly fatal form of cancer. Eight of the victims died less than 24 months after the diagnosis was made.

The cause of the outbreak is unknown, and there is as yet no evidence of contagion. But the doctors who have made the diagnoses, mostly in New York City and the San Francisco Bay area, are alerting other physicians who treat large numbers of homosexual men to the problem in an effort to help identify more cases and to reduce the delay in offering chemotherapy treatment.

· · ·

My neighbour Klaus Nomi was the first person I knew who

died of AIDS. I'd run into him on the stairs going up to our apartments and he could hardly go up the four floors. He rested on each step. I watched as he turned into a walking skeleton. He stopped speaking, as if even words took away his energy. I would bring him apples or apple juice and, if he was too weak to open the door, I'd leave the small packages outside in the hall. But some days I'd hear him singing, 'Lightning striking again and again'. I thought it was a longing for love, but it was a longing for life.

When I told him I'd seen a friend of mine die by being struck by lightning when I was eleven years old, he asked me to tell him the whole story with all the details.

I'd been running across an open field, running from the rain and the sky lit by lightning bolts. I stopped running to look down at my friend, Ginny, who had fallen and was lying in the tall wet grass. The huge discharge of electricity had made her turn completely blue. She died and I wasn't even touched although I was running only a few feet ahead of her.

Klaus asked, 'What was that like?'

I answered, 'It was that kind of luck, you know, unlucky luck.'

A few times a month Klaus would knock on my door, a knock to the beat of Beethoven's Fifth, to give me lemon bars and cookies. He borrowed my make-up.

The night he performed on *TV Party* in his look, which was white pancake make-up with black lipstick, through my bathroom window that opened to his kitchen window, I heard him practicing for hours and hours throughout the day.

The song was 'Mon cœur s'ouvre à ta voix' from Camille Saint-Saëns' opera *Samson and Delilah*. The song is sung by Delilah to seduce Samson, as she wants him to reveal to her the secret of his strength. One refrain in the aria is 'respond to my tenderness'.

More than a dozen times in wails and whispers, I heard Klaus sing 'respond to my tenderness'.

This day is on my list of the saddest days ever lived.

Since AIDS, our outings meant going to clubs and parties and laboratories for a blood test. The word 'negative' was a beautiful word filled with sunlight and a desire to run and run. Suddenly we were all writing, painting and singing about the body and mortality. We wanted our work to overflow with courage and rage.

Jean-Michel Basquiat's paintbrushes, paint sticks or little-kid crayons were swords, daggers and knives.

And there was wit and laughter.

On a wall on Houston Street, between Mott and Mulberry Streets and next to Milano's Bar, the word 'NEGATIVE' was written twenty times.

Next to this was scrawled in black spray paint, 'YOU DIDN'T GO TO THE PARTY OBVIOUSLY!'

Widow Basquiat

Suzanne had long, straight black hair and greenish black eyes and very white skin. Her mother was British and her father was Palestinian. As a child her mother gave her bleaching cream for her skin. Her father had a terrible temper, which was one of the reasons she ran away from home in Canada.

Suzanne and I used to walk the streets looking for Jean-Michel Basquiat, who she loved and who she was breaking up with and getting back together with all the time, or to see who was around to hang out with. Sometimes we'd go to Rammellzee's studio, 'The Battle Station', to look at his robot creatures on skateboards, each skateboard standing for a letter of the alphabet. There was a sign in the studio that said 'He who dies with the most toys wins'. He loved Suzanne and even bought her a pair of shoes at Fayva when he noticed the ones she was wearing were all worn out.

On Thursday afternoons, before our waitressing shifts, we'd go to the Gracie Mansion Gallery or to Patti Astor's Fun Gallery, the first downtown art gallery in NYC that showed graffiti art and brought hip-hop culture into the mainstream white art world. As we looked at work by Kenny Scharf, Keith Haring or Fab 5 Freddy, Suzanne would say 'Interesting', and puff on her red Marlboro, 'Interesting, interesting, very interesting', and puff on her red Marlboro again.

We used to follow DJ Afrika Bambaataa around the clubs. He played at Negril, a reggae club at Second Avenue and 11th Street, Danceteria and then mostly at the Roxy and the Peppermint Lounge. He played soul, jazz and reggae and would create a mood by stopping his records mid-spin and then turn them back and forth. He kept everything unexpected by playing a Latin song and then Led Zeppelin followed by Eddie Money singing 'Baby Hold On', Sly and the Family Stone's 'Stand!' or 'Thank You (Falettinme Be Mice Elf Agin)' and then lots of reggae and electrofunk. Bambaataa was the founder of Universal Zulu Nation, which organised groups, often as an outgrowth of gangs, from the Bronx and New York together as a prideful musical movement. Zulu Nation had Zulu Queen Kenya and Makeba as well as Zulu warriors, leaders, kings and chiefs.

We were big fans of Kid Creole and the Coconuts and we made sure we went to the clubs where they were playing. Coati Mundi, who co-founded the group and played the vibraphone, and Suzanne were always giggling and winking at each other as if winking were kissing. Suzanne and I knew all the lyrics to the songs 'The Lifeboat Party' and 'Stool Pigeon'.

Suzanne was constant in her complaint that her shoes were too small, a legacy from a childhood of poverty. And so, in honour of this, Jean-Michel painted Suzanne in a painting called *Big Shoes*. In the portrait Suzanne looks like a little girl in her mother's shoes and her mother's red lipstick.

I already knew that if you couldn't give someone something, you could write it instead. I was giving away gifts in my poems. Jean-Michel painted Suzanne some big shoes so she'd have them. I wrote her a green parrot so she'd have one.

In 1981, at the time when Rene Ricard wrote an important essay on Basquiat, 'The Radiant Child', Suzanne was no longer working for Rene for a dollar a poem. He'd brought her scraps of things he'd written on napkins, receipts or even squares of toilet paper to type up. When the old typewriter Rene gave her stopped working, Suzanne would iron out these rolled-up-into-a-ball scrap poems by pressing out the wrinkles with her hands and give them to me to type for her.

Rene and I both published our first poems in the *Poetry Project Newsletter* published by St Mark's Church in-the-Bowery, where we went to the Sunday afternoon poetry readings.

My poems from this time are about Rapunzel, museums, the hominid skeletons found in the Shanidar Cave, with titles such as 'Sky of Fish and Premonitions', 'As I Go East,' 'Fifty-Four' and 'Your Hands Remember, Though You Don't'.

The poet James Ruggia was working there and Rene had a huge crush on him. Rene would tell him, 'Come live with me and I'll give you a little room off the kitchen where you can sew and darn your socks.'

In 1993, James married Beverly, my Kingswood Cranbrook boarding school friend.

Rene gave me a copy of his first book of poetry, which was published in 1979 by the Dia Art Foundation with a Tiffany-blue cover. In the introduction, Rene wrote: 'The poems themselves must not be confused with the book that contains them; I am not a writer. I make poems.'

On 22 May 2014, Suzanne and I went to Rene's memorial at the Eldridge Street Synagogue.

Suzanne asked if I remembered any of the poetry we'd typed up.

There was one line that stayed with me: 'My infinitives never split.'

I had poems published in the *Poetry Project Newsletter* and, after Club 57, I read at St Mark's Church. The space still smelled of the devastating 27 July 1978 fire: the steeple was damaged, organ destroyed, a section of the church's roof fell in and nine of the twenty-three stained glass windows were lost.

St Mark's Church was the place where I had the US launch of my memoir *Widow Basquiat*, about Suzanne and her relationship with Jean-Michel, which had been published in 2000 by Canongate, the only publishing house who loved the book after nineteen editors rejected it because they didn't know who Basquiat was and thought that no one would care about his girlfriend. On the back cover of this first edition is one of two portraits my mother painted of Suzanne when she came to visit me in Mexico City in 1994.

At St Mark's Church I read, 'She always keeps her heroin inside her beehive hairdo. The white powder hidden in the tease and spit. The cops can't find it. The drug addicts can't find it.'

And

'Jean-Michel has found Suzanne like a small box, an old coat, a penny on the sidewalk, found a little boy-girl like him. He also knows his skeleton.'

The reading was held on 9 September 2001, a Sunday.

Two days later, the images on television showed the Twin Towers falling down in slow motion again and again, as if they could never stop falling for ever and ever. There were images of doctors on the street, waiting outside all the New York City hospitals for the victims to arrive. All the doctors in the area had to report to their emergency rooms and so Suzanne, who was now a doctor, was called in too.

I phoned her and she said was pacing outside the hospital waiting for the ambulances with doctors but no one had showed up.

'All the doctors and everyone in the hospital knows this is all theatre. We need to be seen here but,' she said, 'nobody's coming.'

'¿Dolor o placer?'

Jean-Michel, of both Haitian and Hispanic heritage, lived with his family in Miramar, Puerto Rico, from 1974 to 1976. He knew about the island's Taíno peoples. Boricua sayings populate his work and the Spanish language filled his canvases: *fuego, flores, peligro, abuelita, milagro, Campeon de boxeo, El gran espectaculo.* His great friend was a fellow Puerto Rican, Al Díaz, with whom he spray-painted aphorisms on the D train of the IND subway line.

In 1981, Jean-Michel painted a white policeman with scary red eyes and the words 'LA HARA' written four times on the left side of the work. '*Hara*' is Puerto Rican slang for 'police'.

When I told Jean-Michel that our childhood USA television shows were dubbed in Mexico, he made me recite them and couldn't believe that Buckwheat, from *The Little Rascals*, was called Perlita in Spanish. Our favourite episodes were 'The Boyfriend and the Teacher' and 'Mrs Jones Is Going to Get Married', and somewhere on a painting I imagine he had to have written Stymie's quote 'Wood doesn't grow on trees', which cracked us up every time.

In *The Addams Family* Gomez always asks Morticia if she wants 'Pain or pleasure?' When I told Jean-Michel the question in Spanish, he wrote it down on a drawing next to the word 'CORNFLAKES'. He also asked me to scribble down the theme song in Spanish for him to memorise.

He was curious to know who my favourite Mexican painter was. When I said it was Hermenegildo Bustos, Jean-Michel grabbed a marker out of the pocket of his jacket and wrote the name down in the palm of his hand.

Charlie Mingus was inspired by Mexico and had even written a jazzy take on Mexico's mariachi bands called 'Los Mariachis' on his album *Tijuana Moods*.

Jean-Michel asked if I knew that Mingus had recently died in Mexico.
'Yes, 'I said.
'He went to see a famous Indian shaman there, who operated on him.'
'Yes,' I said.
'Who was he? Who was this healer?'
'She was Pachita,' I said and told him about my own experience with visiting Pachita.

In 1978, Mingus was operated on by Pachita in Mexico City. At age fifty-six, he was debilitated by ALS and could no longer play his double bass.

After the visit to Pachita, Mingus's wife, Sue Graham, wrote about the experience in her memoir, saying that Pachita 'knows how to cut, just between the pores. From God to Pachita!'

Jean-Michel asked me once about Jesus Bracho, a name he later scrawled down and crossed out in one of his untitled paintings from 1985. Bracho had been in charge of the production design on Luis Buñuel's surreal movie *The Exterminating Angel*, which was filmed in Mexico. Jean-Michel and I could both quote from the movie. It was a game between us.

He liked to remember the scene after everyone wakes up from a long sleep in the living room still dressed in their elegant dinner clothes from the night before: 'These clothes are so stiff they are for statues and not for men especially at five in the morning.'

Then I'd ask, 'What do you eat?'

And Jean-Michel would answer, 'Paper, missy, it's not very appetising, but it serves to trick hunger.'

Polaroids

I have a box filled with Polaroid photographs that have faded. The poisonous odour of the negative that I peeled off and threw away still lingers on the paper.

There are Polaroids of me dancing in a corner with Hal at the Mudd Club.

There are Polaroids Basquiat took, which were given to me by Zoë Anglesey, our mutual friend who was a jazz critic and the jazz editor for Brooklyn's *Ace* magazine. Ravi Coltrane wrote a song for her called 'For Zoë'. Jean-Michel and Zoë liked to talk about music and he said his art was painted jazz.

A month before Zoë's death in 2003, Barbara and I took her in a wheelchair to the Bronx Zoo to visit the gorillas of the Congo Gorilla Forest, which opened in 1999 and was at the time the largest rainforest ever built. It was a dark December afternoon with a wall of snow falling and we were the only visitors. For several hours we watched the gorilla families play, laugh, fight and stare at us, stare into us, through the tall glass walls.

Later, coming back to Manhattan in a taxi, Zoë told us how she'd been Miles Davis's lover off and on and on and off for years. She also told us she had always been unwanted and grew up in an orphanage. This winter trip to the Bronx Zoo to see the gorillas was her goodbye voyage.

Before she died, she gave me a framed set of Polaroids taken by Jean-Michel. They are faded completely and are now only a black-sky square of nothing.

What is there?
Cops in a subway car?
Alba Clemente's hands catching rain?
Maripol's eyes?
Suzanne's mouth?
Jean-Michel's fingers in Suzanne's mouth?

I have other Polaroids I took in 1983, which have also faded completely.

Is there a photo of Suzanne giving a performance at Pyramid when she decided she wanted to be a singer? Suzanne sang 'Summertime' over and over again for an hour. That night Suzanne hired two large men she met on the street as body-guards to stand on each side of the stage as if they were protecting a celebrity.

Is there a photograph of a subway car with the scrawled words 'LET ME PLEASE YOU IN YELLOW'?

Is there a sunset on the beach in Nantucket?

Is there a white police club against the night sky?

Is there a photo of Suzanne's small hand in Michael Stewart's small hand before he left Pyramid on 15 September 1983? Later that night, he was brutally attacked by six white police officers when he was caught spray-painting 'RQS' on a wall of the First Avenue L train Brooklyn-bound subway station at 2.50 a.m. He died after thirteen days in a coma.

La Tulipe

At La Tulipe I worked the coat-check closet for tips and checked the coats of Jackie Kennedy Onassis and Lillian Hellman on many nights, as they dined there together twice a month.

Located on West 13th Street from 1979 until it closed in 1991, La Tulipe was one of the first expensive prix fixe places in New York City. From the coat-check closet and past the small oyster bar I could look in on the dining room, with its dark berry-coloured walls covered in mirrors, and watch Lillian Hellman. She used to smoke and eat at the same time: a puff and a bite a puff and a bite a puff and a bite.

Like a bottle with a message in the ocean, sometimes I placed a typed poem of mine in the pockets of these expensive coats.

As there was free time before the diners finished, paid and came out for their coats, John Darr and I would talk. He and his wife, Sally Darr, the chef who had been one of the senior editors of *Gourmet* magazine, owned the restaurant. Sally was the first serious female chef at a restaurant in New York after Leslie Revsin and La Tulipe was known for its apricot soufflés and red snapper fillet cooked in parchment paper with fennel. John was a Quaker and a founder of the World Council of Peace in 1950 as well as being a member of the United Christian Council for Democracy and American Peace Crusade. In 1953, this background made him a target of the House Un-American Activities Committee. I used to tell him about the US and Mexican communists my father befriended in Mexico and we had philosophical talks about creating change in the world through violence and non-violence.

I was beginning to have some of my first poems published and I asked John about using my mother's name. It was John who said that, more than an act of feminism, Clement was the name I should take because it was ancient and because it meant merciful.

In those days, La Tulipe was one of the most expensive restaurants in New York. Every night before closing we'd count the silverware, which we laid out on a table in the dining room. And every night at least one slender silver coffee spoon had been stolen.

When I came back from Paris I also worked as an intern for Viking Penguin Press, where I was in charge of the slush pile. Money, photos, cheques and threatening letters arrived in the envelopes along with the manuscripts. One day there was a letter from John Hinckley, the man who had tried to assassinate President Ronald Reagan, from St Elizabeths Hospital. He wrote he had an interesting story to tell.

I shared an office with the writer Abigail Thomas, who, between family dramas and calls with Stephen King and Peter Matthiessen, wrote short, beautiful poems. Once, on a busy morning with telephones ringing all around us, she turned to me and said, 'Hey, have you ever noticed that every time you make love to some men it rains?'

My friend Nancy Shore started a literary salon in those days, which I went to with the writer J. B. Miller every other Wednesday night. Nancy's roommate was Whitney Houston's first manager and the singer often came to these nights to hang out and listen to our poems and plays. We used to go and hear her sing at jazz clubs in the city. On one of these evenings, when JB had just returned from a trip to Paris, he gave me a large purple ceramic flower he'd stolen for me from a grave in the Père-Lachaise cemetery.

Walls Were Paper and
Trains Were Books

The graffiti artists called themselves writers and never graffiti artists, which was a term assigned by journalists and art critics.

They'd say 'Let's go writing' or ask 'Are you a writer?' or 'What do you write?'

I would read the walls and subway trains like pages.

There is artistry in how the can of spray paint is used. The aerosol metal needs to be shaken up well so the paint does not drip. The writers call these drips 'tears'. When the paint drips badly it's called 'crying'.

Once, walking down Avenue A past Tompkins Square Park, I read words that wept blue all down a wall. The rounded, balloon letters spelled out: 'HE MAKES ME EAT MEAT'. Under these words was written 'WHY DO FATHERS WALK OUT ON THEIR KIDS?'

I knew Dondi White had been around when *Children of the Grave* appeared on subway cars signed by him. This was many years before he made his large work across the side of three subway trains. *Children of the Grave* was also written before AIDS. These works were so masterful because they were meant to be seen as the train was rushing by, so the letters seemed to be in movement, running away. He was a genius. Dondi did this with no distance to gain perspective, writing two feet away from the train or even between trains in the subway yards.

Dondi and I became friends at the Mudd Club, where we both went to see Sur Rodney (Sur) interview artists on his Manhattan Cable Television, a show held at the club. Dondi did not like clubbing so he'd come by Bandito, the Mexican restaurant where I was a waitress, and hang out. I gave Dondi a poem, which he said he'd write on the side of a subway car for me. I don't know if this ever happened and I don't remember the poem. He had a sweetness that appeared in his work in the unexpected image of a flower, star or a bee. He told me the idea for *Children of the Grave* was taken from a Black Sabbath song: 'Children of tomorrow live in the tears that fall today . . .'

Dondi was a member of the Death Squad, which included Kool Aid 131, Bear 167, Toxic and Mr. Jinx 174, among others over the years. Their work was all over the Broadway number 1 line, tagged with their acronym TDS. They often hit lines 2 and 3. Although they bombed (getting the art up quickly and in as many places as possible) all the time, they were more interested in artistry than bombing and their style included creating wild alphabets, which, on purpose, were difficult to read. Not only did TDS want respect for their skill, they wanted to be known for their risk-taking. There was great danger involved in creating these works: they could be arrested, beaten up or killed.

Jenny Holzer's *Truisms* appeared on walls and were there to be read. She printed up these maxims and glued them to walls and storefronts. I read 'OLD FRIENDS ARE BETTER LEFT IN THE PAST' and 'CONFUSING YOURSELF IS A WAY TO STAY HONEST'.

One summer Jean-Michel, as Samo, wrote all over the Lower East Side. In huge letters across one wall he wrote:

THESE INSTITUTIONS HAS THE MOST POLITICAL INFLUENCE: A. ☐ TELIVISION B. ☐ CHURCH C. ☐ SAMO D. ☐ McDONALDS.

Jean-Michel was in the 'Beyond Words' show organised by the visual artist and filmmaker Fab 5 Freddy and Keith Haring in April 1981. This was the first time that the writing on subways and walls was presented as visual art. Keith Haring, Futura 2000, Kenny Scharf, Rammellzee, Lady Pink and others were part of the show. That night, the Bronx hip-hop scene and East Village New York scene united at 77 White Street on the fourth-floor gallery space of the Mudd Club.

It seemed that on that night everyone came together in a moment that had been coming and would only last a few more years.

Even after Jean-Michel wrote 'SAMO IS DEAD' all over the walls of the Bowery and SoHo, announcing his retirement as a graffiti artist, his work never stopped being work to be read. He was always a writer and some paintings are manuscripts. In his painting *Roast*, with the drawing of Al Jolson in blackface, he writes 'MALCOM X VERSUS ~~AL JOLSON~~' and reading down the canvas are the words: 'BLUE RIBBON', 'NECK', 'COTTON SLAVES', 'NEGRO SPIRITUALS', 'PORK + BEANS', 'ALL BEEF'. In one corner is the iconic shape of a house with an 'S' for Suzanne inside.

D&G Bakery

When six or seven black or blue Cadillac Coupe DeVilles would drive up Mulberry Street, Beverly and I knew that one of the Italian mafia families was having a meeting at the Ravenite Club.

In 1978, Julien Jackson, who was married to Beverly's aunt Mary, the Martha Graham principal dancer, bought the D&G Bakery in Little Italy from Guido Pradella. The bakery had a one-hundred-year-old coal-fired underground brick oven, which had been a German cake oven, and was one of the first bakeries in New York City to sell rustic Italian bread to restaurants.

This may have been the very first time an African American was allowed to do business in the area and Julien had to get permission from the Italian mafia clubs. The bakery oven entrance was on Mulberry Street and the storefront was on Spring. Julien had to ask the Gambino family and they came to an agreement. Julien did not think to ask the Genovese family, as he didn't realise that Spring Street was their territory. They retaliated by setting fire to some of Julien's delivery trucks.

I knew how this worked. It had happened in Mexico to my father's factory.

Julien was a businessman, but he'd also worked for the New York Health Department as a radiation control officer, so he had the knowledge required to understand the science behind breadmaking as well as true respect for Italian craft and tradition. When he needed bakers or staff, he placed help-wanted advertisements in *Il Progresso*, New York's Italian-language newspaper.

Beverly moved to New York City in 1981. Since our days at Cranbrook, we had seen each other frequently either in Mexico or Paris, where she stayed with me for a while. I would spend many afternoons with her at the bakery. Julien took pride in hiring young artists and a vibrant community was formed around the place.

When I was at the D&G Bakery with Beverly, her cousin Jenny and Rachel McDavid, a friend and artist who worked at the bakery for years, we'd look out the storefront window directly at the Ravenite and watch the mafiosi in action. By sitting on the counter inside the storefront, and due to the manner in which the bakery's awning opened, it was easy to watch what was going on in the street without being seen. These men spent most of the time talking outside the club, as they were sure the place was bugged. The street even smelled like their Hai Karate and Old Spice cologne. Many years later we learned that the FBI was trying to figure out ways to place bugs in the parking meters outside the club.

John Gotti was a common presence going in and out of the Ravenite, which was guarded by two black Dobermans. The club was named after Poe's 'The Raven', which was Carlo Gambino's favourite poem.

Constantino Paul Castellano, whom Gotti ordered a hit on in 1985 at the Sparks Steak House, used to appear every now and again. When we looked at Castellano coming and going, we knew he'd made a fortune in concrete, but that he also had a successful poultry business called Dial Poultry that delivered chickens to more than three hundred butchers in New York City. It was common knowledge that Castellano had his daughter's boyfriend killed. The boyfriend had offended Castellano by comparing him to Frank Perdue, who had the other New York poultry business, Perdue Farms. In 2004, this hit, and this reason behind it, was confirmed by a government witness.

Beverly once saw a man she'd been told was a notorious hitman from the Gambino family walk toward the bakery. He was dressed in glossy grey trousers, which almost shimmered, and a tight black turtleneck sweater that showed off his muscles – a hitman look. He was speaking heatedly to a man in an animated way, gesticulating frantically with his hands. When he got under the bakery's awning, the hitman pushed the man against the storefront window and violently pointed his finger right at the man's nose.

The hitman said, 'I fuckin' tol' you to go upstairs and fix my mother's toilet!'

Another time Beverly was locking up the bakery after dark and, as they walked by, she heard this same hitman man say to the man walking with him as he gestured toward her, 'Yeah, she's black but she's okay.'

An Incident on the Way
to a Borges Reading

On 2 October 1982, I went to hear Jorge Luis Borges read. As I was early, I went into a bar with a view of the street and had a glass of red wine. A handsome man, who said he was from Russia, came over and sat beside me. He asked to read my palm. I opened my hand and he looked at the lines with care. He said, 'If you're afraid of loneliness, don't marry. That's Chekhov.'

At the lecture, Borges said, 'All poetry consists of feeling things as being strange.'

Once I had graduated from NYU, I worked at Times Books, which was a division of the *New York Times*, as an editorial assistant. I met Robert O'Neill at Times Books, where he also worked while he was getting an MFA at NYU. He was the brother of a food writer for the *New York Times* as well as a brother to a Yankees right fielder who became a five-time All-Star and five-time World Series champion. Robert was a wonderful writer with a big Irish heart, which he gave over to everything he did. His wit and the solace in his poems could have out-written most anyone.

We spent the summer of 1983 in Nantucket together, working at a restaurant. In the morning the fishermen brought the bluefish in to the back kitchen door. They were about three feet long, lying one on top of the other in a red plastic bucket. Robert laid one of them on the kitchen counter and with a large thick knife and hammer taught the young kitchen helper how to cut up the fish. Robert cut off the head and then, in pieces about one inch and a half thick, he cut down the fish's body, using a hammer on the knife to crush through the vertebrae. I loved watching him in those moments when he was far away from me.

Once, when he was shucking an oyster, he found a tiny pearl. He had a ring made for me with the pearl.

Robert memorised poems. He'd recite Dickinson, Lowell and Snodgrass and say he needed to educate me away from Latin American and British poetry.

We broke up, in essence, because I wanted to live in Mexico and he wanted to stay in the USA. During my years in New York City, I never expected to stay. As every other Mexican abroad, from the richest to the poorest, we're all thinking about Mexico.

A few years later, after I was back living in Mexico City and about to be married, Robert wrote me to wish me well but also wrote, 'You should know this, I don't have any former loves. I cannot quit loving people.'

It was Robert's engagement ring, with a teardrop-shaped diamond, that I later used to pay the printer in Mexico for my first book of poems.

Night-time Phone Calls

A grassroots centre to support women who had been raped or were victims of violence, which was established and run by a group of women volunteers, was under the apartment I lived in when I moved from St Mark's Place to 14th Street. The federal Violence Against Women Act was not passed until 1994, more than a decade later.

The women who worked at the centre asked if I would watch over the night-time phone calls. This meant that every day at five o'clock the telephone was passed out of their window and I would reach way down and take it up into my window with the cable still attached to the rape centre's jack.

Every policeman in the country knows, the volunteers told me, that the worst night of the year for violence against women was Super Bowl night. On that night they did not give me the phone and two volunteers spent the night camped out downstairs.

I had a list of questions I had to ask if someone were to call needing help. The first question was: 'Are you safe now?' If they said they were not safe, I'd tell them to call 911 or I'd call 911 for them. In most cases, I took down their information and the next day one of the volunteers would follow up on the call.

In my notes from these calls, the words 'maybe', 'perhaps', 'might' and 'possibly' were used again and again, as if experience were tentative:

I think perhaps my arm is broken.
Maybe I was raped. He is my husband.
Possibly I have a concussion, I can't see anything.
Perhaps he had a knife. I'd never seen him before.
Maybe my children saw something.
I might be unable to walk.
He'd been stalking me for days. Can you hear me?
    Maybe I'm whispering.

I Say to You Goodbye

I expected a yellow taxi, but Suzanne picked me up in a black limousine. She was wearing a huge black straw hat, which was almost like wearing an umbrella. I wore a long silk black blouse over blue jeans and a blue-and-black Mexican rebozo with large Mexican earrings from Oaxaca.

There were so many taxis and limousines outside the Mary Boone Gallery, our driver could not get close and we had to get out and walk for two blocks. There was a very long queue, but there was a doorman who was letting in celebrities.

Every now and again, Jean-Michel would look out the door at the crowd outside trying to get in. When he saw Suzanne and the big hat, he broke into a joyful smile and instructed the doorman to let us in. Jean-Michel led us to one side of the crowded gallery where his mother, Matilde, was sitting all alone in a small roped-off section. She was dressed simply in a black dress and flat black shoes. She had a deep forever-worry line between her eyebrows. Jean-Michel ordered Suzanne and I to stay with her. We never left her side.

Matilde, Suzanne and I sat in a row of three chairs, as if we were sitting in a church pew. Matilde, who was an artist and had schooled her son on art and taken him to museums as a child, was quiet.

At seven years old, Jean-Michel was playing in the street and was hit by a car. He broke his arm and had internal injuries and had to undergo a splenectomy. At the hospital, Matilde gave Jean-Michel *Gray's Anatomy* to read. He later used these anatomical drawings as inspiration for his paintings. He called his musical band, which he called his 'noise band', Gray, after the book.

From our chairs and to our right we could see *Brown Spots*, Jean-Michel's enormous portrait of Andy Warhol depicting him as a huge yellow banana – a tribute to Warhol's album cover for *The Velvet Underground & Nico*. A few months later, as if they were in a duel, Andy paid him back by painting Jean-Michel as Michelangelo's *David*.

In the gallery, on the wall to our left, was *Deaf*, a deep-red-and-white painting of a man playing a harp under the words: 'BLIND HARP PLAYER'.

Suzanne and I wondered if Matilde was over-medicated that night or simply overwhelmed by her son's fame, as she hardly moved in her chair and didn't speak. Even when she greeted us, she only bowed her head down gracefully. Matilde answered our questions in monosyllables.

Suzanne, 'Isn't this wonderful?'
Matilde, 'Yes.'

Jennifer, 'I've never been to Puerto Rico, but I'm from Mexico.'

Matilde said, 'Ah, sí, México.'

The crowd walked by and stared at us. Every now and again someone we knew would wave. We were part of the show.

The small and elegant cream-coloured, nineteen-page catalogue of the exhibit contained six full-colour plates, a black-and-white photograph of Jean-Michel and a poem by A. R. Penck. It was called 'Poem for Basquiat'. The poem opened with the line, 'I say to you hello' and ended with, 'I say to you goodbye.'

I say to you goodbye.

Many years after Jean-Michel died, Suzanne and I went to visit Matilde at her small and modest house in Brooklyn. She didn't seem to know who we were, although she was kind and gracious and served us lemonade in a coffee mug.

Four Paid Mourners

Robert, Lili and Robert's brother, who was Lili's boyfriend, and I worked one day as paid mourners. I'd seen a sign at the Actors' Studio at NYU requesting actors to be mourners at a funeral in Long Island. The pay was $45.

I wore my Gloria Swanson black velvet dress and Lili wore an elegant cream-coloured suit and a box hat with a veil covering her face. Robert and his brother wore suits and ties. We drove out to Long Island in the moving truck he and his brother had bought for their one-truck-only moving business in the city. The four of us were crammed in the front seat.

The church had only about ten mourners in the light-brown wooden pews and we wondered if they were being paid as well. The four of us sat together and solemnly went through the funeral service, bowing our heads and looking very serious. When we walked out, a lady standing stiffly at the door handed each of us an envelope containing our forty-five dollars.

As we were in Long Island, we decide to go to Jones Beach. The young men whipped off their ties, took off their shoes and socks and rolled up their trousers. Lili and I slipped out of our shoes and peeled off our stockings. As we walked toward the water, I said, 'Everyone falls in love and gets their heart broken – if they're lucky.'

We knew these love affairs were ending. For an hour or two we walked the white sand coastline in our mourning clothes, in mourning for each other.

'Headless Body Found
in Topless Bar'

In 1983, Lili began her unique line of greeting cards made to look like the front page of the *New York Post* and based on its headline 'Headless Body Found in Topless Bar'. Her bestselling card was one for Christmas with the news, 'Fat Man Found Dead in Chimney, Eight Reindeer Starve on Roof'.

Lili was hired by the owner of Bandito, where I worked with Suzanne, to be the restaurant's creative director. Along with Chazz Petersen, who was one of the members of Watchface, Lili created installations and interactive performance art several times a month. They also created fashion nights called 'Look Like a Mannequin' and 'Wear What You Never Dare to Wear'.

The conceptual artists David McDermott and Peter McGough almost always came to these nights. They had decided to live as if they were in the late 1800s and dressed as fine gentlemen in long morning coats, detachable collars and top hats. Their rundown townhouse on Avenue C, on the Lower East Side, was furnished with antiques and they had no electricity and lived by candlelight. Sometimes they were driven around the Lower East Side in a horse-drawn carriage.

One of their paintings was called *When Touring the Louvre, American Sailors Attract Considerable Attention by Being Handsome* and was dated 1914. Their motto was 'We've seen the future and we're not going.'

Because Bandito closed at four in the morning, it quickly became a place to go to late at night. The owner allowed us to give away free drinks, so this too made it a happening place. Bandito was one of the first places to serve huge frozen margaritas. In Chinatown, Lili bought bags filled with a menagerie of plastic animals and mermaids, which the bartenders attached to the side of the tall margarita glass or placed on the snowy surface.

We played the hip-hop song 'Beat Bop' over and over again for months. We'd put down everything we were doing and dance around the empty restaurant. 'Beat Bop' was a rap single recorded by Rammellzee, K-Rob and Al Díaz. Jean-Michel produced the song and designed the cover. Dondi gave me a copy, as it was being given away to everyone like candy.

Get funky in the place!
Get funky in the place!

On many nights Lili would sit with me while I would be cleaning up the place at five in the morning. We would drink cognac in large balloon glasses and listen to Maria Callas singing *La Traviata*, as a kind of exorcism from the pop, hip-hop and new wave that we'd played loudly all night. Our music mixed with the sound of the garbage truck and street sweeper outside.

And while we were closing, across the street at the Second Avenue Deli, Abe Lebewohl was opening the doors and letting in his cooks and cleaners. Next door was the Sigmund Schwartz Gramercy Park Chapel, where we could watch bodies arriving in the early morning as well as the winding down of a nightly, and we thought illegal, poker game. This funeral parlour had held the services for Ethel and Julius Rosenberg. For a few minutes, as the day dawned, the Lower East Side seemed like the 1800s in the grey light with the first stirring.

Abe Lebewohl was a beloved man in the neighbourhood. At the deli he hired survivors of the Holocaust, who were very old men and women with the tattooed numbers from extermination camps on their arms. Many did not speak English. He also fed the homeless. Every night there would be a long line of people, even some women with small children, lined up at the back of the restaurant for food. If the line went around the block, they'd make it back to the front of the restaurant, where the sidewalk was covered with stars of New York's Yiddish theatre, like the stars in Hollywood for great actors. They stood waiting for bread and soup on the stars of Molly Picon, Menasha Skulnik and Fyvush Finkel.

My sister worked as a waitress at Bandito and then became the manager and Abe and Barbara became good friends. They spent a lot of time together, going back and forth between Bandito and the deli, and very often they were working on ideas to help the neighbourhood. Abe used to say that he and Barbara should build an underground tunnel between the two restaurants so they wouldn't have to spend the whole day crossing Second Avenue. In 1996, Abe was murdered on the way to the bank to make a deposit. This crime has never been solved.

Once, shortly after this, I was at Bandito with Barbara, remembering Abe, when she pulled a piece of embroidery out of her bag, placed it on her lap and began to stitch. It was a patterned cotton cloth of two poinsettias fixed to an embroidery hoop, which had been bought at a stand at the San Ángel market years ago. Barbara had carried it from the sewing classes we used to have with Chona on Calle Palmas, to my mother's house after my parents' divorce, to boarding school and to New York City. She'd carried the unfinished sewing as if it were a thread leading her away from the Minotaur.

Decades later, at a literary festival in Mexico, which was held in the port city of Tampico in 2004, Barbara and I met the writer Hugo Claus, who'd written *The Sorrow of Belgium* and was also known for being a part of the CoBrA art movement. Barbara and I soon realised that Claus was in an advanced stage of Alzheimer's, as he'd only packed a book and a shirt and even needed our help to understand how to open his suitcase. Claus was confused the whole time and was lost on two occasions, after which Barbara became his constant companion and was cited as his wife in all the Mexican periodicals.

In these days, Barbara and I became the seamstresses out of a fairy tale. Before Hugo Claus returned to Belgium, Barbara and I went to the Tampico market and bought needles, small scissors and blue and white thread.

We then spent Hugo's last afternoon in Mexico, before he was to take his flight back to Europe, sitting with him in his room, which overlooked a view of the port stretching out to the dark-blue waters of the Gulf of Mexico. We told him about our sewing and embroidery classes and how, as girls, a seamstress used to come to our house to make our clothes. Barbara and I sat side by side for two hours and sewed his honorarium of $9,000 cash into the seams and pockets of the trousers and jacket he wore to travel back to Belgium.

Refrigerator

Barefoot and dressed in a black Armani suit, white shirt and tie, was the way Jean-Michel posed for the 1985 cover of the *New York Times Magazine*. This was the moment Suzanne felt left behind and knew she had to honour her intelligence. This was the spark that would become her life as a medical doctor with a specialty in psychiatry.

Suzanne decided to sell her refrigerator that was covered in Jean-Michel's scribbles, a skull with teeth and the word 'TAR' written twice. We'd used it as a closet for years and at some time I had scrawled my name in the bottom right-hand corner with a brown marker. She asked my boyfriend Robert if he could take the refrigerator to Sotheby's in his truck all the way from 1st Street to 72nd.

Suzanne and I cleaned out the refrigerator and scrubbed it down with soap and baking powder before it left Suzanne's apartment.

Andy Warhol bought it for $5,000.

In 2010, Suzanne and I, and other friends of Basquiat, went to the Basquiat show in Basel. It was the year Jean-Michel would have turned fifty years old.

Suzanne's refrigerator, covered with Basquiat's scribbles and words, was in a small room of its own at the back of a gallery.

As we contemplated the refrigerator in the cold and reverent gallery space with a white sign beside it that said 'DO NOT TOUCH', protected by alarm wires and a museum guard, Suzanne and I turned to look at each other, really look at each other.

It was as if our whole lives were being protected behind the velvet rope. It was as if the refrigerator still contained our lives through the objects we imagined still rested within the cold white interior.

Behind the rope, watched over by a guard, inside that refrigerator with Basquiat's scrawls all over it, and which we used like a closet, I could see my poems and books, Suzanne's chemistry exams and biology notes and the bracelets, drugs and apples.

I said to her, 'No one would have bet on us.'

In Memory of Joan

On 5 February 1985, Suzanne had her one-woman show at the rundown Vox Populi Gallery at 511 East 6th Street between Avenue A and B. Her paintings of George Washington as a black man on a dollar bill and the cartoon figures of Black Dagwood and Blondie, as well as large portraits of Malcom X and Muhammad Ali, covered the walls. Alone on one wall right at the entrance was her portrait of Joan Burroughs with an apple on her head, which I had watched her paint for weeks as I wrote my true confession stories.

It was a tiny space and the gallery filled up quickly. Lili told me that two members of the Guerilla Girls had arrived, who she was sure were the ones who went under the nicknames Frida Kahlo and Hannah Höch. The Guerilla Girls were formed that year as a response to the MoMA show 'An International Survey of Recent Painting and Sculpture' with a roster of 165 artists that included only 13 women. I was always sure that Lili was a Guerilla Girl. Dressed in their gorilla masks, the Guerilla Girls protested the lack of women artists in museums and galleries. Lili always had inside information, which she'd tell me followed by, 'Forget what I just said.'

Barbara and I went to Suzanne's show in long capes like high-waymen, made for us by Maria Del Greco, who lived next door to Suzanne on 1st Street.

Andy and Jean-Michel arrived in a black limo, but they never came inside. They stayed out in the car looking at the art opening through the car window. This made Suzanne so upset she didn't even realise she spent the rest of the night walking on tiptoe, as if this kind of walk could suddenly make her fly right out of the window and into the New York sky.

The show sold out.

Suzanne gave me the painting *In Memory of Joan*.

The afterparty was at Indochine.

As a present to Suzanne for her birthday that year, I gave her a copy of my romance novel *Desire Among the Statues*, which I'd written while she was painting and had just been published. We'd had so many laughs about the text, and when I'd been paid the $500 for the book we went on a shopping spree at Fiorucci and spent it all. This romance novel was about a love affair with a sculptor in Florence. Decades later, when I met a sculptor in Florence, and even as we shook hands for the first time under the shadow of an ancient tower, I knew I was experiencing that rare occurrence when coincidence and desire meet.

I also gave Suzanne a typed copy of the first poem I wrote about her, with the lines:

We are two women nestled in the grape of each other,
for all this we understand: in some African places
women still marry trees. She draws starved men
shooting arrows into branches . . .
And at dawn, when finally she sleeps,
her body round, ear-shaped in the cove of her bed,
she wears the names of African girls: Small Fish,
Pretty Arm, Hanging Bee, Spilled Water.

Packing the Bags

I packed two books. One was Andy Warhol's *Index (Book)* from 1967, which he had given to me. The book has a pop-up airplane inside, a paper disc with the words 'THE CHELSEA GIRLS' and a portrait of Lou Reed. And I also packed a first edition of W. B. Yeats's poems, signed by the poet, which was given to me by a Polish man who owned a secondhand bookstore on Third Avenue.

I flew back to Mexico.

I brought back my ballet pointes.

I brought back the rings on my fingers and the rhinestone bracelet of leaves Hal gave me as a present for my twentieth birthday.

I brought back the stolen purple ceramic Père-Lachaise cemetery flower for my garden.

I brought back Suzanne's painting, *In Memory of Joan.*

Since Burroughs' *Queer* had been published in 1985, I now knew that William Burroughs had walked the Mexico City streets crying on the day of Joan's death. Afterwards he realised that, as everything is foretold, he'd been grieving for Joan even before he killed her. From *Queer*:

It was about three o'clock in the afternoon, a few days after I came back to Mexico City, and I decided to have the knife sharpened. The knife-sharpener had a little whistle and a fixed route, and as I walked down the street towards his cart a feeling of loss and sadness that had weighed on me all day so I could hardly breathe intensified to such an extent that I found tears streaming down my face.

'What on earth is wrong?' I wondered.

Jean-Michel Basquiat
1960–1988

I was in Mexico City when Jean-Michel died. Suzanne wrote me a letter on 19 August 1988 to say she was devastated and had looked for the poem I'd written for her, as she wanted to read it at his memorial. She wrote that it was so painful because the new people in his life at the end didn't know her. Because of this, she explained that she desperately searched for some confirmation to find herself and that my poem was most comforting.

Jean-Michel died of an overdose of heroin. He'd tried desperately to stop but just could not. Suzanne wrote that the sadness would stay for ever and thanked me for always honouring her love for him.

'You are one of the few who dared to understand it,' she wrote.

Nine years later, I wrote *Widow Basquiat*.

One of the last times Suzanne saw Jean-Michel was at the Great Jones loft he'd rented from Andy Warhol. She told me that he was so thin he seemed transparent. He stumbled when he walked and fanned himself constantly with his hands. Suzanne said there was a painting lying against the wall on which Jean-Michel had written in oil stick 'MAN DIES' four times. It was a death foretold. The prophecy seemed to even be there when he'd painted the cemetery in 1980 in his work *Bird on Money* in honour of Charlie Parker. On the work are the words 'GREEN WOOD' and 'PARA MORIR'.

We never went to the Green-Wood cemetery in Brooklyn to place flowers on his grave, but years later on a whim we visited the grave online at findagrave.com, where we found the graves of both mother and son.

JEAN-MICHEL BASQUIAT 1960–1988
SECTION 176,
LOT 44603

MATILDE *ANDRADES* BASQUIAT (1934–2008)
UNMARKED GRAVE

And Fate's
Third Chance

If it is true that you have three chances to meet your fate, I was given three chances to find Aline.

Aline had given up dancing professionally and was mostly living in Paris but she would come back to Mexico for long spells. On my return to Mexico, we would meet in Cuernavaca and visit Waldeen and go to Aline's parents' house. Aline's mother, Ruth, was almost always there and she liked to recount the stories about Frida and mentioned the time when Walter Pach, a famous art critic, had come to Mexico to meet Frida. Even though she should have liked this, Frida got away from him as fast as she could and asked Ruth and her sisters to place a blanket in the bathtub where she lay for an hour or so until Pach had left. Ruth recalled Frida asked the sisters to bring her a whisky and made fun of Walter Pach's moustache. Frida said that there were many kinds of moustaches but that his was 'unbearable because it was like a heavy rain shower'.

Ruth told us that at one time in her life she was feeling very depressed and so her father took her to see Frida, whom he knew could solve the problem, and left her at Frida's house for many hours. Ruth said Frida told her things that were taboo for girls to hear.

When Aline and I asked her what these things were, Ruth answered, 'Well, you know, this and that.'

Many afternoons, after lunch, Aline and I liked to lie on blankets in the grove of magnolia trees to one side of the garden and drink coffee to the sound of bees swarming in and out of the giant flowers.

I told Aline I always miss the places I have not been to, the people I never knew, the men I did not love, the children I did not have. I miss the tree that did not give me shade, the scent of a yellow rose I did not pick and being a man in armour and the moment he can rest in battle. This sense of absence is so great, I miss the people I'm with and the water I'm drinking.

I told Aline, 'I will always miss you. And even this is so true, I miss you when I'm with you.'

Aline Davidoff Misrachi 1957–2017

Return

In New York City no one believed I was going back to Mexico. But this was all I wanted.

I went back to Mexico's particular kind of rebellion, which is really anarchy, founded on the knowledge that everything is lost.

Back to Mexico, where we feel closer to the dead than to the living.

I went back to eat bride cake, have two children and a brief marriage.

After my wedding, my dress was worn by Lili to marry her first husband in Mexico and then Silvia wore it too. We shared it as if we were in a Grimms fairy tale called 'The Three Brides and One Dress'.

The dress has a rip in the lace at the hem from getting the garment caught under my high heels while dancing.

The garment was also forever filled with the hyacinth scent of Sung, Lili's perfume.

And the white gown is stained with Silvia's red Dior 999 lipstick at the collar along a tiny strip of lace.

At Silvia's wedding, which was held in her garden in San Ángel, her mother did not sit at the bride and groom table. She sat at the back behind the tall and ancient jacaranda tree with all her gardeners.

The never-washed wedding dress is in my closet in a small black suitcase.

I went back to Mexico and the promise that fireflies will return to the gardens, the promise of winning the lottery, the promise of a miracle, and where no one ever sweeps up the party confetti.

Permission Credits